© Naumann & Göbel Verlagsgesellschaft mbH, a subsidiary of
VEMAG Verlags- und Medien Aktiengesellschaft, Cologne
www.apollo-intermedia.de

Complete production: Naumann & Göbel Verlagsgesellschaft mbH, Cologne
Printed in Poland

ISBN 3-625-11125-X

Indian Cookery

NAUMANN & GÖBEL

CONTENTS

A COLOURFUL MELANGE

The Products of India

Indian cooking is like a mysterious, aromatic melting pot filled to the brim with fine culinary art. Influenced by a natural diversity of religions and cultures boasting 14 languages and more than 100 dialects, India is not just a country but more like a continent. The potpourri of cooking styles contains elements ranging from the exotic to the simple, from the traditional to the modern, and from the regional to the international. Discover this cuisine of contrasts, discover culinary India!

A Cuisine full of contrasts – a culinary journey across the Indian sub-continent, from the Himalayas to Sri Lanka

Full of unique character and exotic mystique, many Europeans already enjoy Indian cuisine with its variety and nuances. Indian cooking is a magical aromatic melange of regional specialities, time honoured traditions, religious diversity and western and Arabic influences. These elements compliment each other to make up a very individual and versatile kind of cuisine. In India you can truly experience the pure knowledge of multicultural cooking. The cuisine is accordingly characterised by this rich mixture. A cook's creativity is highly regarded in Indian circles and his recipes are usually passed on by word of mouth with the spices playing a central role. Indian housewives are also proud to take up the challenge of making even the simplest of dishes in a variety of ways with differing combinations of spices to give them a whole new flavour every time.

Meal times are a ritual in Indian society and play a very important part in daily life. Unlike in Europe the kitchen in India is the focal point of every household, where the whole family meets to communicate. All day long pleasant aromas drift out of the kitchen whetting the appetite for the shared meal to come. Made up of many dishes that compliment each other not only in their flavour but in their appearance as well, the portions are served simultaneously on bowls or plates. The *thali* – a large metal tray – is traditionally used for the presentation of the dishes. These are served in small bowls known as *katoori*. A main dish as

such does not exist in Indian cooking; instead each individual can put a meal together to his or her heart's content. Another aspect that enriches the character of Indian cuisine is that although it strongly upholds traditional methods, it is still not hesitant to accept new ways and unknown influences.
In many cases meals are now eaten with a knife and fork instead of the fingers. The entire meal is still served all at once, but now an extra clean plate is usually offered with it.

The most outstanding characteristic of Indian cooking, however, is still that it is based on numerous styles of cuisine directly from India itself. The number of regional varieties is considerable, and we can only touch upon the vast pallet of specialities and curiosities.

The North
Kashmir with its fertile valley and Punjab as the "cornfield of India" are both famous for their opulent cuisine that is marked by a distinct Persian influence. Fruits, vegetables and nuts thrive in the temperate climate. The world famous basmati rice grows here amongst other types of cereal. Kashmir itself boasts a multitude of rich meat and poultry dishes. Like the people of north China, rice is eaten in abundance. The main source of nutrition is wheat, and this is utilised in various forms from whole grains to flour for making the famous Naan and Chapati breads.

The West
Particularly hot and fiery dishes come from Goa in India's western regions and have a marked Portuguese influence. Chilli, vinegar, coconut milk, and tamarind juice are

frequently used in the cooking here. The small minority group of Christians, who are also a reminder of the Portuguese ruling settlers, still eat pork. On the coast near Bombay, however, fish and seafood feature prominently on the menu. A speciality of the region is the well-known *Bombay duck*, which is in fact a silvery kind of fish that is dried and baked.

Central India
The influences of Persian cooking reach right into central India, and the resulting cuisine is considered to be one of the finest in the land. The Mongolian style is also very extravagant, rich and imaginative. Mild aromatic spices like cinnamon, cardamom, nutmeg and clove are used to give a delicious taste to meat dishes, which are mostly prepared with lamb. Beef, on the other hand, is preferred in areas with a predominantly Muslim community. The popular rice biryanis and pilau are spiced with saffron and turmeric to give the dishes their unmistakable bright yellow colour.

The East
Bengal and Bihar form the east coastal and river regions of India and are naturally rich in fish and seafood. Mustard seeds, aniseed, cumin and fenugreek seed are typically added to dishes here, giving the tasty aquatic produce a wonderful, mildly sweet taste.

The South
The further you go southwards in India, and the higher the temperatures climb, the hotter and spicier the dishes become. Staunch devotees of Hinduism live here, and according to their religion the consumption of meat in general, and

beef in particular, is prohibited. In this region rice and vegetables are therefore consumed in abundance. The dishes are mostly spiced with hot chilli peppers, but there are milder ones using coconut milk.

Ayurveda – The knowledge of life

Indian cuisine is widely considered to be the cradle of vegetarian culinary art. This, on one hand, takes its origins from Hinduism, which is the dominating faith in India and prohibits the eating of meat, which the majority adhere to. On the other hand a simpler, more practical reason is that vegetarian ingredients on a day to day basis are within the means of the average person and meat is simply too expensive.

India's culinary culture is based upon the knowledge collected over thousands of years that eating is not only a source of nutrition but linked directly to ones well being. In China the cuisine is based on the principles of Yin and Yang, where two poles are opposite yet in harmony with each other. In India the fundaments of their cuisine come out of Ayurveda.

This holistic "Knowledge of life" teaches that together with other important elements, the correct form of nutrition upholds an internal harmony and helps you to achieve and maintain a balanced and healthy body, mind and soul.

In not so many words ayurvedic cuisine tastes good and heals at the same time. The methods used for combining foods and prepara-

tion techniques are particularly unique and is very much oriented toward the individual and his or her taste and constitutional orientation. Food is not prepared in a general way for everybody but each tasty dish is tailor made to the individual depending on his or her ayurvedic type. Each recipe has been handed down over the years and is prepared accordingly. The selection and combination of ingredients is even made according to factors like the temperament, seasonal changes and weather conditions.

If you are interested in a more in depth study of the ayurvedic art of cooking there is a large source of literature available on the subject in most book retailers.

Herbs and Spices – more than just aroma and flavouring

Nothing is more strongly associated with Indian cooking than its aromatic herbs or the bright, multicoloured array of its spices that in return give the Indian dishes their typical exotic fiery hot or mild flavours. The western world consumes a great many ready-made spice mixtures and the variety of preparations is on the increase. The individual flavourings and seasonings therefore are becoming more and more insignificant. How great then in contrast is the tempting, tantalising and diverse world of Indian cooking, where the seasoning of the food is considered to be the absolute highest form of art for every meal.

An Indian cook will usually have more than 20 different spices at his or her disposal to help in mixing the appropriate blend that will match and enhance the dish in question. Unlike our cooking methods, where spices are used individually, in India each single spice is carefully blended with others to lend a dish a particular flavour. The spices are prepared in such a way that unleashes their full power and flavour. The combinations you can create are endless, making each colourful mixture a mastery of the senses and a pleasure to select.
Follow us down "the road of dreams and into the world of exotic spices"! Discover the treasures of India that over the millenniums gave rise to great conquests and which made many an emperor, king or prince, and even entire nations rich and powerful. These days the possession of spices from overseas does not hold the same wealthy status, and has become a normal commodity in most homes. Indian spices are available in many markets, well-stocked supermarkets, and health food shops and of course specialist Asian product traders.

Not only are fresh and dried spices used in Indian cooking, but also fresh garden herbs. New blends are continuously being devised out of different combinations and preparations. The kind of dish being prepared dictates which herbs and spices are to be used and whether they are left uncut, roasted, fried, or ground. Whatever the dish the right blend of seasoning will always enhance the flavour of its ingredients and mark it with an unmistakable aroma. *Masalas*, for example have become particularly well known all around the world and are a mixture of ground spices worked into a paste with water or vinegar.
Herbs and spices are not only used to make a meal particularly tasty but are known for containing healing properties. Using certain herbs correctly you can prevent or cure problems such as flatulence, heartburn, an unsettled stomach or indigestion. Other herbs on the other hand give off special aromas that can have sudorific or cooling effects. These and other physiologically beneficial effects have been known for many years within Indian culinary tradition and it is out of this knowledge that herbs and spices have been combined to perfection bringing harmony to our palates. Introducing certain herbs or spices that are known for their "cooling" effect, without in so doing covering up or losing the main flavour can for example neutralize a hot and spicy dish.

Herbs

Herbs are perfect for giving a meal its aroma and colour and if possible should mostly be used fresh. They guarantee for a healthy and balanced diet and not only in Indian cuisine. At best you should plant your own small herb garden. It is always possible to make some space for the most commonly used herbs, whether it is in your window box, on the balcony or in a small garden.

Fresh herbs can be kept in a sealed container for approximately 2 to 4 days, much longer when frozen. A clever solution to keeping herbs fresh is to finely chop them up, mix them with a little water and then pour the mixture into the cube sections of an icemaker and freeze. Just let them melt into your hot sauce whenever needed.
You can make a flavouring paste by coarsely chopping and mixing the herbs and stirring them into a good olive oil. If stored in a fridge the paste will keep for 8 to 10 days. The herbs should always be kept well covered with oil. You can add any herbs and spices of your choice to a good oil and thus have special homemade flavoured oil always at hand.

Particular favourites in Indian cooking are the healthy herbs basil, green coriander and mint, which enhance dishes with a certain kind of freshness.

Basil – Tulsi
Basil has a strong, slightly bitter taste and a strong aroma. This domestic herb has differently sized leaves, whose colour varies from light May green to violet. You can use all kinds – even thai basil when it comes to Indian dishes.

Green coriander – Hara Dhania

Green coriander is as popular in Indian cooking as is parsley in ours. The strongly fragrant, somewhat bitter, small leaves are easy to grow from seed. The seeds themselves and even the roots are frequently used as a spice as well.

Mint – Podina

Mint – also known as peppermint – is mostly known for making tea. Depending on the type, the leaves can be smooth or wavy with fine hairs but always with a strong menthol fragrance. In the Indian and oriental cuisine mint is often used to add the very unique exotic taste that we often associate with these dishes.

Fresh Spices

Chilli Peppers – Hari Mirch

Chillies are the pods of the capsicum pepper plant. How hot or mild they are depends on their colour – red, green, or yellow (in descending or-der). A rule of thumb is: the smaller the hotter. It's the seeds that make them so hot. Removing them will therefore result in a milder dish.

Garlic – Lassan

In north Indian cooking garlic is used mostly in combination with ginger and onion. This member of the onion family has a very strong flavour and is either loved or hated by many. One thing is for certain – it has earned a great deal of respect for its numerous healing properties and effectiveness as a natural antibiotic. If the taste is too strong for you however, an alternative is spring garlic.

Lemon grass – Bhustrina

This perennial aromatic grass has a stem with a fine lemon flavour, which slightly lessens when dried. Lemon grass grows everywhere in India, but its use as a spice is particularly common in the cuisine of north and central India.

Onion – Peaz

The onion is also preferred in north Indian cuisine. The piquant sharp, bulbous lily plant is the most famous cooking ingredient in the whole world, and like garlic has very good health maintaining properties.

Root Ginger – Adrak

Ginger is a bizarrely shaped root from a tropical lily plant. The hot and spicy flavour unfolds itself best when you freshly grate the silky light brown coloured bulb. The roots can be kept fresh by storing them in sandy moist soil.

Spices

Spices are extracted from the dried out parts of a plant e.g.: the leaves, seeds, rind, buds, stems, roots, etc. Their full aroma and flavour unfolds itself when they are roasted and then ground and depending on the recipe, cooked separately from the ingredients or simultaneously and later stirred in with them. Stored whole in a sealed container spices will stay fresh for a long time. They should only be ground or grated shortly before use.

Anise – Soaf

Anise (aniseed) is the seed kernel of an umbel plant. Indian cuisine and Far East cuisines do not usually make a distinction between aniseed and fennel, which has a similar taste, and that is why both spices are given the same name in India. The seeds have a sweet spicy taste. We use them mostly for teas and for baking at Christmas time, but in Indian cooking the seeds lend vegetables and meat a fine and piquant flavour. They are also a good digestive stimulant.

Asafoetida – Hing

Asafoetida is dried resin from the roots of an umbel plant. It has a black brown colour and an intense, bitter burning taste, which is very potent. That is why asafoetida is used very sparingly in Indian cooking.

Bay (leaves) – Tej Pata

Bay leaves have a bitter balsamic taste. The Indian bay leaves look different from, and are much cheaper than, the dark green leathery leaves of the evergreen bay shrub that grows in the Mediterranean. In cooler regions this attractive plant can be grown in large pots and is very practical because the leaves can be picked and used all year round.

Cardamom – Elaichi

Cardamom pods are the dried fruit of the cardamom shrub. The reddish brown seeds contained inside have a sweet spicy flavour. You can buy green unbleached or white bleached pods, or just the seeds and in the ground form as well. If you cook with the pods they should be removed before serving.

Cayenne pepper – Lal Mirch

Cayenne pepper is derived from grinding dried red-hot chilli peppers. You can mostly buy it ready ground, not in its pure form however, but usually mixed with added marjoram, garlic, caraway. The Hungarian hot and spicy rose paprika powder is just as good for using in Indian dishes.

Cinnamon – Dalchini

Cinnamon is derived from the inner bark of the cinnamon tree. The light brown coloured sticks have a fine spicy flavour. Cinnamon is particularly good for meat and rice dishes giving an extravagant piquant taste. It is opular not only in Indian cooking – where the spice is exported from Sri-lanka – but also highly regarded in Arabic cooking. The sticks are usually added whole and then removed after cooking and not eaten.

Cloves – Laung

Cloves when fresh have a strong pink colour. It is only when they are dried in the sun that they get their typically brown coating. They are cooked whole and removed from the dish before it is eaten.

Coriander – Dhania

Apart from using green coriander as an herb, the plant is also dried, ground and used as a spice in India. Coriander belongs to the family of umbel plants. The seeds have a piquant spicy taste and are a base ingredient to a lot of Indian cooking. Only buy a small amount of seeds and grind or grate them shortly before use, because they quickly lose their flavour.

Cumin – Djira

Cumin is one of the most important spices in Indian cooking and is very similar to our indigenous caraway seeds – at least in appearance. The taste however is bitter and spicy with a slight camphor–like aroma. Its characteristic intense after-taste is not to everybody's liking.

Fenugreek – Methi

Fenugreek is a multifaceted plant. Not only are the fresh leaves used as a vegetable but the dried seeds are also used as a spice and even as medicine. The fine leaves, when they are fried in ghee or in oil, unfold a fine aromatic flavour it and is ideal for mixing with vegetables or pulses. The seeds have a piquant, bitter taste and are the ingredient for many seasoning powders and pastes.

Liquorice – Multhi

In India liquorice is more regarded for its painkilling properties than as a spice. According to Ayurvedic teachings a natural substance exists for every existing ailment and it was with this in mind that this blossoming plant root was discovered. The small unspectacular looking pieces of wood have a aniseed like taste and are found in most delicatessens or specialist markets. It is not recommended to chew or consume liquorice if you suffer from heart or kidney problems or are pregnant.

Mango (powder) – Amchor

The tropical mango fruit originally comes from India but is now grown all over the world. These days you can buy them fresh nearly all year round. In Indian cooking the fruit is used for seasoning either in its green unripe form or dried and ground into powder. Mango powder will give a dish a spicy and sour edge and is a good alternative to lemons.

Mustard seed – Rai

The best-known mustard seeds are a whitish colour and have a mild flavour; the black seeds however taste very hot. In Kashmir and Bengal they are lightly fried in oil and meat as well as vegetables are added and stewed. The biting aroma gradually fades during cooking and a piquant-sweet flavour remains. Sweet mustard mixed with peanut or sunflower oil can also be used as an alternative.

Nutmeg blossoms – Javita
Nutmeg – Jaiphal

The blossoms and nut kernels come from the fruit of the nutmeg tree. The nutmeg blossoms or Macis are taken from the fleshy part of the seed. At harvest time they are carefully removed then airdried and flattened. The orange-brown blossom is a speciality amongst seasonings and is far more aromatic and stronger than the nutmeg, which is the dried seed kernel of the apricot sized fruit. You can buy the light brown coloured nut whole or ready ground. The strong smelling and somewhat bitter taste is far more intensive when freshly ground than in powdered form but loses its taste quickly.

Pepper – Pippali

Pepper in all its forms has been used for hundreds of years on the Indian sub-continent as a seasoning or remedy for many ailments. It is considered to be one of the oldest and most sought after produces in the world. The berries of this evergreen climbing shrub are green to start with, then orange and finally turn a strong red colour. Unripe green peppers are harvested and preserved in salt or vinegar brine. White pepper powder is in fact made from the yellowy-green berries that are picked shortly before ripening. The fleshy fruit is removed and the seed kernel washed and laid out to dry and bleach in the sun. The resulting taste is milder than the more commonly used black pepper. Although also harvested unripe, it is then directly fermented for a few days and finally put out to dry until slightly shrivelled and brownish-black in colour.

Poppy seeds – Khus-Khus

Poppy seeds are best known in Europe as an ingredient in baking. In India however the black and white

seeds are often used in cooking and lend the dish a lovely strong nutty taste. The white seeds are different because they contain opiates whereas black seeds do not.

Tamarind – Imli

Tamarind is a dark brown, fleshy and very sour tasting husk, and is used in many dishes to give a piquant-sour touch. Before using take a fermented flat piece of tamarind and place it in boiling water for 15 – 25 minutes, continuously pressing it down until it is soaked through. The juice is then pressed out through a fine sieve. As you can see preparing Imli needs a lot of effort. For a similar taste and quicker solution try a squirt of lemon.

Turmeric – Haldi

Turmeric is a member of the ginger family. The spice is extracted from the bright orange root bulbs of the plant and has a mild ginger like flavour is used. Being much cheaper than saffron it is a good alternative in giving the dish an intensive yellow colour.

ABC of Indian cooking

We could fill page upon page outlining the basis of Indian cooking which counts as one of the worlds most diverse. Instead we have selected a few of the most important terms, special ingredients, culinary secrets, kitchen utensils and cooking methods to arouse your interest for the fascinating culinary art of this country.

Chenna – quark

Chenna is comparable to our cottage cheese, and looks similar to quark. Paneer is the name given to pressed chenna and both are often added to main dishes and as the basis for some desserts. The preparation is very long-winded and difficult and only makes sense if your diet is predominantly Indian. Otherwise use cottage cheese as a substitute.

Dahi – yoghurt

Most of the yoghurt in India is made out of buffalo milk, which is much creamier and richer than the yoghurt produced here. To get similar tasting results you can instead use natural full milk yoghurt mixed with double cream.

Dals – Pulses

Dals form the nutritional basis for many vegetarians in India and are their main source of protein. Beans, peas and lentils are available in all types, colours and sizes. They are used whole, husked or unhusked, coarsely ground or worked into flour. Just as numerous are the recipes for Dals, so you will never get bored with them.

Ghee – clarified butter

Apart from vegetable oil, Ghee is mainly used for cooking. The use of animal fat is taboo for religious rea-

sons. True that butter is an animal product, but it is allowed because the animal does not have to give up its life for it. Ghee is available in most Asian shops but you can easily make it yourself. Cut some unsalted butter into small slices and melt in a pot on a low heat. Let it briefly boil and then reduce heat quickly and cook until the butter foam turns yellow. Pour the resulting liquid through a clean kitchen towel and leave to cool. The clarified butter will keep some months in the fridge.

Kebabs or Kababs

Kebabs as they are more commonly known are made with marinated meat, poultry or vegetable balls. They are first grilled or fried and then braised in a sauce.

Nariyal – coconut

In India coconut is used mostly freshly grated, or in liquid form as

a sweet cream or unsweetened milk. It is used a lot in cooking particularly in the south. You can buy it ready made in Asian shops. It is worth buying it fresh however because when grated shortly before cooking it is much juicier and stronger in flavour than the ready made dried flakes. Take care to test the coconuts' freshness before buying by shaking them to see how much liquid is inside.

Pappadams – wafers

Pappadams are round crispy wafer thin snacks and are sold everywhere in India in sizes ranging from 6 – 26 cm. They are deep fried in oil and the dough expands to twice its size when cooked. To prepare the dough is very complicated and time consuming and they are therefore normally bought as readily seasoned dried round wafers.

Roasting

Roasting Indian style is a special

cooking technique taken from the earlier north Indian and Mongolian kitchens. The seasoning is first fried separately in butter or Ghee and then the remaining ingredients added. Finally some liquid is added and the temperature lowered, allowing the ingredients to stew in their own juices. Originally the lid would have been sealed with dough, placed in hot ashes and covered in glowing coals. The modern way is much easier however but also needs time. Everything is baked in an oven at 120 – 160 °C.

Tandoor – Indian clay oven

A Tandoor is an oven made of clay and set into the ground with an opening on the top. Bread is baked in the hollow of the oven by sticking it to the smooth sides. When baked through it will fall down. Also the famous meat, poultry and fish tandooris are cooked inside this oven. The preparation for the tandooris is very important. The meat or fish is marinated until it turns an unmistakable red colour. Wood or electric grills are just as effective for cooking.

EXOTIC MAGIC

Masalas, Chutneys and Pickles

The secret of Indian cooking lies in the innumerable herbs and spice blends known as Masalas. Each one is prepared and mixed especially to fit the dish and varies from region to region. Chutneys and pickles are made from fruit and vegetables and have an unmistakable sweet and sour taste. They give a little extra flavour to even the simplest of recipes and are a typical side dish at Indian meals.

Curry powder

Curry is India's most famous blend of herbs and spices. It is always prepared using several types of seasoning and every Indian has their own personal blend.

Coriander

The light brown aromatic coriander kernels have a slightly sweet, piquant taste, and are a permanent fixture in the Indian kitchen. It is added to practically every meal.

Black peppercorns

Black peppercorns are the unripe berries of a climbing shrub, which have been dried in the sun. They taste stronger than the white ones.

White peppercorns

Roasting the berries until their fleshy parts come off leaves white corns, which are then dried in the sun or by machine.

MIXED SPICES

Curry powder

7 tbsp coriander corns
2 tbsp cumin seeds
2 tbsp fennel seeds
2 tbsp fenugreek seeds
2 tbsp caraway seeds
1 tbsp yellow mustard seeds
1 tbsp black peppercorns
10 cloves, 10 dried red chillies
4 dried curry leaves
1 tbsp chopped lemongrass
4 tbsp ground cumin

Preparation time: approx. 10 minutes
295 cal/1239 kJ

■ How to do it:

Roast all the ingredients in a frying pan without using fat and then grind down to a fine powder. Fill into a tightly sealing jar and store in a cool dry place.

1 Roast the ingredients in a pan without using fat.

2 Grind down the mixture to a fine powder.

Garam Masala

5 tbsp each: cardamom, coriander, and caraway seeds
4 tbsp each: black and white peppercorns
20 green cardamom pods
3 cinnamon sticks, 12 cloves
1 tbsp freshly ground nutmeg
1/2 tbsp saffron

Preparation time: approx. 15 minutes
295 cal/1239 kJ

■ How to do it:

Roast all the spices apart from the nutmeg and saffron in a frying pan without fat, until all the corns turn light brown. Allow it to cool down and then grind down mixture finely. Add nutmeg and saffron, mix everything together and store in a tightly sealed container in a cool and dry place.

1 Roast everything together in a frying pan.

2 Allow to cool and then grind down finely.

TOMATO-DATE CHUTNEY

Serves 4

14 oz (400 g) dates
1 lb 5 oz (600 g) tomatoes
3 tbsp freshly grated ginger
1 Spanish onion
2 cloves of garlic
4 tbsp peanut oil
1–1 1/2 tsp each: ground
cumin, fennel and cardamom
2 tbsp ground cloves
2 tbsp brown cane sugar
2 cinnamon sticks
2 bay leaves
salt
cayenne pepper
1 tsp turmeric
5 tbsp raspberry vinegar

Preparation time: approx. 45 minutes
432 cal/1816 kJ

■ **How to do it:**

Wash the dates and tomatoes and
chop into small pieces. Mix in the
ginger. Peel the onions and garlic
and chop up finely. Heat up the
oil in a pan and gently fry onions
and garlic. Add the dates and
tomatoes. Then add the ground
cumin, fennel and cardamom fol-
lowed by the ground cloves, sugar,
cinnamon, bay leaves, salt, pepper
and turmeric. Flavour with the
raspberry vinegar and simmer for
approximately 25 minutes. Remove

the cinnamon sticks and bay
leaves, fill small bowls with chutney
and serve.

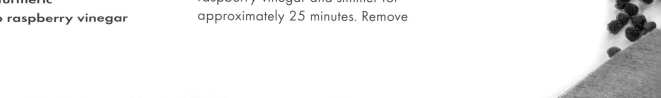

LIME PICKLE

Serves 4

12 limes
3 tbsp garam masala
2 tbsp sea salt
1 tbsp cumin seeds
2 tbsp crushed black
peppercorns
1 tbsp cayenne pepper
9 fl oz (250 ml) sunflower oil
9 fl oz (250 ml) lemon juice

Preparation time: approx. 15 minutes
(excluding 12 days marinating time)
745 cal/3129 kJ

■ How to do it:

Wash the limes in hot water and cut
into quarters. Place in a bowl and
sprinkle spices over them. Mix the
oil and lemon juice together and
drip over the limes. Cover completely with a kitchen towel and leave to
marinate for 12 days (in the sun if
possible) until the limes have soft-
ened. Stir occasionally and make
sure the limes are always covered
with liquid.

Limes

Unlike lemons the peel on limes is
green and thin, and the fleshy interior
greenish-yellow. Also popular in
Asian and Caribbean cooking.

Lemons

Lemons are generally bigger than
limes with thicker yellow peel and
yellow flesh. Remove the bitter white
pith before eating. Lemon peel is
also known for its uses in European
cooking.

COCONUT SAMBAL

Serves 4

10–11 oz (300 g) coconut flesh
4 cloves of garlic
3 green chilli peppers
2 red chilli peppers
1 tbsp grated ginger
4 tbsp coconut milk
salt
3 tbsp lemon juice
2 Spanish onions
3 tbsp peanut oil
1 tbsp black mustard seeds
4 curry leaves
3 tbsp ground cumin
2 tbsp ground turmeric

Preparation time: approx. 40 minutes

392 cal/1648 kJ

■ **How to do it:**

Cut the coconut flesh into small pieces. Peel the cloves of garlic and press them. Wash the chilli peppers and half them to remove seeds and then cut into strips. Add the garlic, chillies and ginger to the coconut and drip the coconut milk, salt and lemon juice over it. Then purée the mixture using a hand-blender. Peel and cut the onions in to cubes and fry them gently in some heated oil. Add the mustard seeds and curry leaves. Sprinkle with the cumin and turmeric and cook until the mustard seeds burst. Leave to cool. Stir in the coconut mix and store in a cool place.

Turmeric

An exotic spice famous for its strong yellow colour and strong flavour that is similar to ginger. Turmeric is the base ingredient to all Indian curry powders.

1 Cut the coconut flesh into small pieces.

2 Half the chilli peppers.

3 Purée the coconut mixture with a hand blender.

4 Gently fry everything in a pan.

CARROT AND CABBAGE PICKLE

VARIATION

For a more southern flavour instead of the carrots and cauliflower try adding mini aubergines that are characteristically violet coloured.

Serves 4

12 oz (350 g) each carrots and cauliflower
16 fl oz (450 ml) Asian stock
8 cloves of garlic
14 fl oz (400 ml) peanut oil
2 tbsp freshly grated ginger
2 tbsp ground turmeric
3 tbsp garam masala
cayenne pepper
1 tbsp each: ground mustard and fenugreek seeds
3 tbsp white wine vinegar

Preparation time: approx. 30 minutes
(excluding 2 days marinating time)
928 cal/3896 kJ

■ How to do it:

Clean the carrots, peel them and cut into slices. Clean the cauliflower and break into florets. Heat the stock, add vegetables and blanch for about 4 minutes. Remove the vegetables and drain. Peel the cloves of garlic and chop up finely. Fry gently in oil for about 4 minutes. Then add the vegetables, ginger, turmeric, garam masala, pepper and mustard and fenugreek seeds together with the white wine vinegar and allow to cook for 4 minutes. Finally fill some jars with the mixture, cover with a cloth and leave in a warm spot to marinate for 2 days. Occasionally shake.

FRESH MANGO CHUTNEY

Serves 4

2 mangos
1 red chilli pepper
3 oz (80 g) cashew nuts
1/2 bunch coriander
1/2 bunch mint
1/2 tsp ground turmeric
1/2 tsp ground coriander
salt
pepper
curry powder

Preparation time: approx. 25 minutes
165 cal/695 kJ

■ How to do it:

Wash the mangos, cut in half, remove stone and cut into strips. Wash the chilli peppers, cut in half, remove seeds and cut into strips. Chop the cashew nuts coarsely. Wash and dry the coriander and mint, pluck off the leaves and chop up finely. Add the mangos, chillies, cashew nuts, coriander, mint, turmeric and coriander to a bowl and purée with a hand blender. Add the salt, pepper and curry to taste. Serve together with meat or vegetable dishes.

Smooth Peppermint

Smooth peppermint, also simply known as mint, is a very popular seasoning in India. Its fresh taste has a cooling effect for main dishes.

Rough Peppermint

Rough peppermint is not as strong in flavour as smooth peppermint. Also known as horse mint it grows on swamps and meadows.

Cinnamon

Cinnamon sticks are the dried bark of the evergreen cinnamon tree. Used very often in Indian cooking they add a fine spicy and piquant flavour to the dish.

Ginger

Ginger is a strangely formed root from a tropical water plant. In Asian cooking it is grated or used in pieces as a universal flavouring.

MINT FRUIT RELISH

Serves 4

7 oz (200 g) fresh peppermint leaves
2 pears
7 oz (200 g) gooseberries
7 oz (200 g) plums
4 tbsp lemon juice
3 tbsp fine sugar
5 green chilli peppers
3 tbsp freshly grated ginger
2 tbsp each: coriander and cumin seeds
8 green cardamom pods
2 cinnamon sticks
peppermint, cinnamon sticks and lemon slices to decorate

Preparation time: approx. 30 minutes

105 cal/441 kJ

■ How to do it:

Wash and dry the peppermint, and pluck off the leaves. Peel, wash and cut the pears in half, remove middle part and chop into pieces. Wash, dry, and cut the plums in half, removing stones and then chop into pieces. Mix the peppermint leaves and fruit pieces together with the lemon juice and sugar. Wash the chilli peppers, cut in half, remove seeds and cut into strips. Add to the fruit mix and purée with a hand-blender. Roast the ginger, coriander, cumin and cardamom in a heated pan without oil. Allow the blend to cool down and then grind. Add the cinnamon sticks and let them infuse for 5 minutes. Remove the cinnamon before serving. Decorate the finished relish with peppermint, cinnamon sticks and lemon slices.

1 Remove stones from halved plums.

2 Roast the ginger, coriander, cumin and cardamom in a pan.

3 Allow spices to briefly cool and then grind down.

4 Add ground spices to the fruit purée.

THE DAILY BREAD

Flat breads, Pasties and other Baked Snacks
In India they do not like to pass through a day without eating their bread. Typically it is flat bread that is prepared in every region and named differently. Chapati, Parathas, Naan and Poori are the most commonly known. Samosas are also a well-loved kind of pasty, the filling of which has hundreds of varieties, as do the baked snacks with their crispy outer crust and soft delicious centres. Many of these recipes originate from the lively and creative kitchens dotted along the streets of India.

CHAPATI BREAD

Serves 4

**9 oz (250 g) each: wholemeal
and wheat flour
3 tbsp ghee or olive oil
2 tsp salt
flour for rolling
ghee or butter for baking
butter to spread**

Preparation time: approx. 25 minutes
(excluding cooling time)
272 cal/1144 kJ

■ **How to do it:**

Mix the flour, 18 fl oz (500 ml) water, ghee and salt and work into a
smooth dough. Knead with wet
hands on a flour-covered surface for
about 5 minutes. Roll the dough into
a ball, wrap in cling film and leave
approximately 30 minutes to cool.
Divide into 16 portions and roll out
flat on a floured surface to a small
pitta bread size. Melt the ghee or
butter in a pan and add chapatis
cooking on either side for 2 minutes
or until light brown spots appear.
While roasting occasionally press
down on bread with the back of a
palette knife. Place fresh chapatis
in dry kitchen towels to keep warm.
Spread with butter before serving.
Chapatis go well with pickles, meat
dishes and soups.

PANKORAS – DEEP FRIED VEGETABLES

Serves 4

7 oz (200 g) chickpea flour
4 oz (100 g) wheat flour
1 tbsp salt
1 tbsp chilli powder
3 tbsp garam masala
1 tsp baking powder
2 green chilli peppers
3 tbsp chopped green coriander
3 tbsp ghee or peanut oil
2 Spanish onions
20 spinach leaves
4 medium-sized potatoes
oil for deep frying

Preparation time: approx. 25 minutes

580 cal/2436 kJ

■ How to do it:

Mix the flour, with 1 pint (600 ml) water and add the salt, chilli powder, garam masala, and baking powder then knead into a smooth dough. Wash the chilli peppers, cut in half and remove seeds, then chop up finally and fold into dough together with the coriander and ghee. Peel the onions and chop into rings. Wash and dry the spinach. Wash the unpeeled potatoes thoroughly and cut into slices. Run the vegetables through the dough and deep fry until golden brown. Place on kitchen paper to remove excess oil, serve on a plate together with a relish of your choice.

Green coriander

Coriander, also known as Cilantro or Chinese parsley, is highly regarded in Indian cooking. You can buy this piquant-aromatic, slightly bitter herb in good shops almost throughout the year. You could also buy coriander seeds and quite easily grow your own.

Chickpeas

The chickpea is a versatile pulse used as an all-rounder in Indian cooking. They are either used whole or ground into flour.

SAMOSAS – PASTIES

Serves 4

10–11 oz (300 g) wheat flour
1/2 tbsp each: ground cumin
and cardamom
1 tsp baking powder
3 tbsp ghee or olive oil
3 tbsp yoghurt
1 tsp sea salt
10–11 oz (300 g) chicken
breast fillets
8–9 oz (250 g) potatoes
8–9 oz (250 g) frozen peas
1 red chilli pepper
2 green chilli peppers
3 tbsp ghee or lard
2 tbsp garam masala
1 tbsp yellow mustard seeds
1/2 tbsp salt
1 bunch fresh coriander
flour for rolling
corn flour for brushing

Preparation time: approx. 40 minutes
(excluding baking time)
740 cal/3108 kJ

Yoghurt

Yoghurt is particularly used in Indian cooking to neutralise the hot spicy dishes. Usually made from buffalo milk it has a rich creamy taste. If you cannot find this simply use double cream.

■ **How to do it:**

Mix the flour with 7 fl oz (200 ml) water and add the cumin, cardamom, and baking powder together with the ghee, yoghurt and sea salt and work into a stretchy dough, then leave to stand for 25 minutes. While waiting wash and dry the meat and then chop into small pieces. Cook the unpeeled potatoes in salted water for approximately 12 minutes. Heat up the peas in salted water for about 3 minutes. Wash the chilli peppers cut in half, remove seeds and cut into strips. Drain the potatoes and peas. Melt the ghee and fry the meat in it. Add the potatoes, peas and chilli peppers. Season to taste with the garam masala, mustard seeds and salt. Wash and dry the coriander and chop up finely and add as well. Let mixture stand for a further 4 minutes, to cool down. Pre-heat the oven to gas mark 4, 350 °F (180 °C). Roll the dough out on a flour covered working surface. Cut out approximately 20 circles each with a 5 inches/12 cm diameter. Cut the circles in half and use a tablespoon to put a portion of the filling on each half. Brush the edges with the cornflour and water and fold over the dough and press down on edges. Bake on the middle shelf of the oven for approximately 30 minutes. Halfway through baking turn the pasties over. Samosas can also be deep fried if you prefer.

1 Cut 20 circles out of the dough.

2 Cut circles in half.

3 Put a portion of the filling on each semi-circle of dough.

4 Fold over dough from one side and press down.

PARATHAS

VARIATION

To give the parathas a little extra kick, use a filling of leek, tomato, garam masala, garlic and a little ginger.

Serves 4

7 oz (200 g) each: wholemeal wheat flour and wheat flour
2 tsp salt
1 tbsp each: onion and celery seed
2 tbsp chopped celery leaves
flour for rolling
8–9 oz (250 g) ghee or butter

Preparation time: approx. 25 minutes
(excluding waiting time)
785 cal/3297 kJ

■ How to do it:

Mix the flour with 14 fl oz (400 ml) water and add salt, celery leaves and work into a stretchy dough. Allow to stand for 20 minutes. Divide dough into 16 portions and roll each out onto a floured working surface into a flat circle of (approximately 5 inches/12 cm diameter). Brush on both sides with melted butter and fold over twice into small triangles. Then brush the parathas with butter again and fry in hot butter on both sides for 3 minutes. Serve warm.

KACHORI WITH PEA FILLING

Serves 4

14 oz (400 g) wholemeal
wheat flour
1 tsp salt
1 tsp each: cumin and aniseed
seeds
1 each: red and green chilli
peppers
3 tbsp peanut oil
1 tbsp freshly grated ginger
5 oz (120 g) frozen peas
oil for deep frying

Preparation time: approx. 40 minutes

680 cal/2856 kJ

■ How to do it:

Mix the flour with 12 fl oz (350 ml)
water and salt and knead into a
smooth dough. Roast the seeds in
a pan without oil, and then grind.
Wash the chilli peppers cut in half,
remove seeds and chop finely. Braise
the vegetables and chillies together
on a low heat. Add the ginger and
thawed out peas to mixture and
press together with a fork. Roll the
dough into balls and push down in
the middle to make a hole and fill
these with pea purée. Close off with
some more dough. Heat oil in deep
fat fryer and cook balls until golden
brown. Serve the kachori while hot.

Habaneros

Habaneros are one of the hottest chillies, and should therefore be handled with gloves and used sparingly.

Red chilli peppers

These small paprika shoots are the hottest of the chilli peppers. Many an Indian dish can thank them for their fiery-hot taste.

Green chilli peppers

Green chilli peppers are somewhat milder than the red ones, the seeds and white flesh inside should be removed however as these can also make them hot.

Light green chilli peppers

The light green chilli peppers are usually larger than their spicy red and green counterparts. They are particularly good for stuffing and taste somewhat milder.

DOSA

Serves 4

4 oz (100 g) red lentils
8–9 oz (250 g) natural rice
1 bunch spring onions
1 bunch coriander
1 each: red and green chilli peppers
1 tbsp freshly grated ginger
1 tsp salt
2 tbsp olive oil
lard for frying
mango chutney, to spread

Preparation time: approx. 25 minutes
(excluding standing and soaking time)
325 cal/1365 kJ

■ **How to do it:**

Put the lentils and rice into two separate bowls, cover with water and leave to soak for approximately 1 1/2 hours. Drain the water thoroughly and liquidise separately with a hand-blender. Trim and wash the spring onions and chop up finely. Wash and dry the coriander and cut leaves into strips. Wash the chilli peppers, cut in half, remove seeds and chop up finely. Mix half of the spring onions, coriander, ginger, chilli, salt and oil with rice and half with the lentils and work into a malleable dough. Leave to stand for 30 minutes. Melt the lard in a pan and add portions of the mix, frying them into small pancakes. Serve with mango chutney for spreading.

1 Put the lentils and rice into two separate bowls, cover with water.

2 Drain the water and liquidise separately with a hand-blender.

3 Work all into a malleable dough.

4 Melt the lard in a pan and fry small pancakes.

MEAT ROLLS IN BATTER

Serves 4

7 oz (200 g) lentil flour
4 oz (100 g) rice flour
1/2 tbsp salt
1/2 tbsp chilli powder
2 tbsp curry powder
1 tbsp baking powder
3 tbsp chopped mint
3 tbsp ghee or peanut oil
1 lb 5 oz (600 g) shoulder of lamb (boneless)
6 shallots
3 cloves of garlic
3 assorted chilli peppers
10–11 oz (300 g) okra (fresh or tinned)
3 tbsp garam masala

1 egg
oil for deep frying

Preparation time: approx. 40 minutes
295 cal/1239 kJ

■ **How to do it:**

Mix the lentil and rice flour with 1 pint (600 ml) water, salt, chilli, curry and baking powder and mint and ghee. Stir together to a smooth dough and allow to stand for 25 minutes. While waiting wash and dry the meat and cut into cubes. Peel shallots and also cut into cubes. Peel the garlic cloves and chop finely. Wash the chilli peppers, cut in half, remove seeds and chop up finely. Drain the okras into a sieve and chop coarsely. Mince up the meat, shallots, garlic, chillies and okras finely and knead in the garam masala and the egg. Roll mixture into small sausage shapes, and then drag through dough. Heat up the oil and deep fry rolls until golden brown. Allow the excess fat to drip off and serve with tomato chutney.

NAAN BREAD

Serves 4

1 lb 14 oz (850 g) wheat flour
1 tsp baking powder
1 small packet of dried yeast
salt
1 egg
7 tbsp natural yoghurt
3 tbsp ghee or butter
9 fl oz (250 ml) milk
2 tbsp poppy seeds

Preparation time: approx. 35 minutes
(excluding standing time)
813 cal/3413 kJ

▇ How to do it:

Mix the flour, baking powder, yeast, salt, egg, yoghurt, and 2 tbsp butter and milk together and work into a smooth dough. Allow to stand in a warm place for approximately 1 hour. Preheat the oven to gas mark 4, 350 °F (180 °C). Knead the dough once again and then divide into 8 portions. Roll each piece into an oval shape. Brush one side with water and placed this side on a greased baking tray. Brush the topside with melted butter and sprinkle with poppy seeds. Place the naan dough in the middle of the oven and bake for approx. 11 minutes or until slightly risen and light brown. Instead of the poppy seeds try onion seeds to give the naan another flavour.

Poppy seeds

The small blue-black seeds of the poppy plant have a distinctive nutty taste and are very popular in Indian cuisine.

Onion seeds

Onion seeds are not as well known as poppy seeds in our cuisine. They can usually be bought at any good delicatessen or health food shop.

SOUP SPECIALI-TIES AND SIDE SALADS

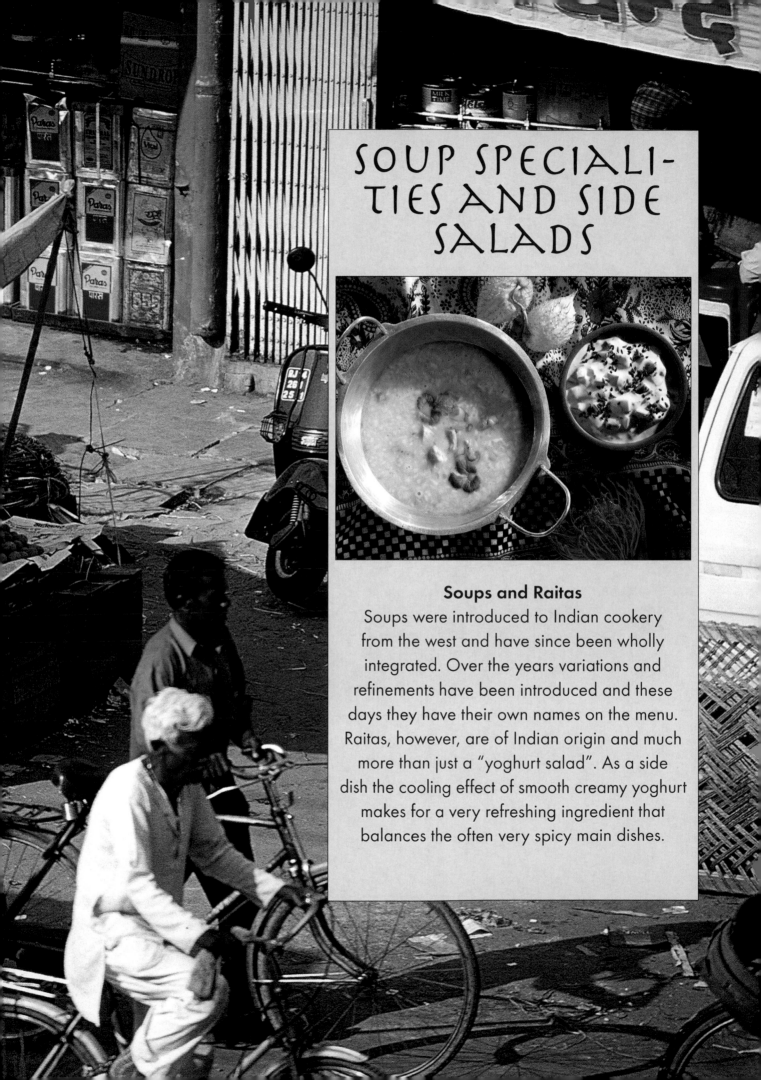

Soups and Raitas

Soups were introduced to Indian cookery from the west and have since been wholly integrated. Over the years variations and refinements have been introduced and these days they have their own names on the menu. Raitas, however, are of Indian origin and much more than just a "yoghurt salad". As a side dish the cooling effect of smooth creamy yoghurt makes for a very refreshing ingredient that balances the often very spicy main dishes.

SPICY CHICKEN SOUP

Serves 4

3 tbsp garam masala
2 bay leaves
1 tbsp crushed pimento seeds
2 lb 3 oz (1 kg) chicken breast with skin
8 king prawns
40 macadamia nuts
6 shallots
3 cloves of garlic
1 piece of fresh ginger (3 cm)
1/2 tsp each: ground turmeric and chilli powder
4 tbsp peanut oil
4 oz (100 g) mung bean sprouts
1 large potato
salt
pepper

Preparation time: approx. 1 hour
990 cal/4158 kJ

Macadamia nuts

Macadamia nuts are the fruits of an Australian tree, similar to the chestnut. They were named after the English explorer, Dr John McAdam. Very similar in taste to the coconut they are used in Indian cooking not as a replacement, but to accompany coconut flesh.

■ How to do it:

Bring 2 pints 13 fl oz (1 1/2 l) of water with the seasoning to the boil. Wash the meat and add it to the broth. Reduce the heat and simmer for 30 minutes. Wash the king prawns and add to chicken 8 minutes before the end of cooking time. When cooked remove both and drain. Put the broth to one side. Remove the bones and skin from the chicken and cut remaining meat into cubes. Peel prawns, remove innards and also cut into cubes. Coarsely chop nuts. Peel the shallots and cut into cubes. Peel the cloves of garlic and chop up finely. Add the nuts, onions, garlic, and ginger to a jar with some of the broth in it and liquidise with a hand blender. Season with the turmeric and chilli powder. Heat up half of the oil in a large saucepan, add paste to it and cook for at least 2 minutes. Add the chicken and prawns and pour the rest of the broth into the pan. Stir in the bean sprouts. Wash the potatoes and cut into wafer thin slices. Heat the rest of the oil in a pan and fry the potato slices until golden brown and sprinkle with salt. The soup now only needs some salt and pepper to taste and can be served garnished with the potatoes.

1 Remove bones from chicken meat.

2 Liquidise rest of ingredients with a hand blender.

3 Fry the paste in hot oil.

4 Pour the broth over everything.

KASHMIR STYLE RAITA

VARIATION

You can vary this traditional yoghurt salad by trying other vegetables in place of the tomatoes and spinach. E.g. 1 medium sized aubergine and 7 oz (200 g) chopped okras fried and prepared in the same way.

Serves 4

1 1/2 lb (800 g) spinach leaves
4 shallots
3 cloves of garlic
1 tbsp fresh grated ginger
4 cherry tomatoes
3 tbsp sunflower oil
1 tsp each: coriander and chilli powder
1 bunch fresh coriander
7 oz (200 g) natural yoghurt
3 tbsp double cream
1 tsp salt
7 oz (200 g) cottage cheese, to garnish

Preparation time: approx. 20 minutes
320 cal/1344 kJ

■ How to do it:

Wash and dry the spinach. Peel the shallots and cut into cubes. Peel the cloves of garlic and chop up finely. Mix the shallots, garlic and ginger together. Wash and dry the tomatoes and cut them into thin wedges. Heat the oil and gently fry the shallots together with the garlic. Add the spinach and tomatoes. Season with coriander and chilli powder. Wash and dry the fresh coriander, cut the leaves into strips and add. Let everything steep for 4 minutes. Mix the double cream into the yoghurt and add salt to taste. Dress a plate with portions of the spinach mix and pour yoghurt over it. Garnish with cottage cheese and serve.

THICK TOMATO SOUP

Serves 4

1 Spanish onion
3 cloves of garlic
4 tbsp peanut oil
1 lb 12 oz (750 g) tinned
peeled tomatoes
3 tbsp garam masala
1/2 tbsp brown sugar
1 bunch fresh coriander
1 pint 10 fl oz (800 ml)
vegetable stock
6 tbsp coconut cream
salt
pepper
1 tsp chilli powder
1 tsp ginger powder

Preparation time: approx. 25 minutes
283 cal/1187 kJ

■ How to do it:

Finely chop up the onion and cloves
of garlic and gently fry in heated
oil. Add the tomatoes with their
juices, garam masala and sugar.
Wash and dry the fresh coriander
and pluck off the leaves. Also add
to the tomatoes and simmer for
about 3 minutes. Add the stock and
cook for a further 10 minutes. Pierce
the tomatoes with a fork and stir in
coconut cream. Finally season to
taste with salt, pepper, ginger and
chilli powder. Serve with flat bread.

Spanish onions

Belonging to the diverse leek plant family, the Spanish onion can be found in many different shapes, sizes and tastes. Most common are the white and red medium strength cooking onions.

Shallots

Shallots are also known as ash leeks and have a mild taste and are therefore considered to be one of the finer onions.

Vegetable and silver onions

The large, mild vegetable onions are particularly good in salads and also good to stuff. The mild, small silver onions are mostly known in a pickled form.

Spring onions

Spring onions also know as leek onions, as the name suggests they are planted in early summer and are a useful all-rounder for salads or cooked with vegetables.

INDIAN PEA SOUP

Serves 4

6 red onions
4 cloves of garlic
2 red chilli peppers
2 green chilli peppers
4 tbsp ghee or lard
3–4 oz (80 g) tamarind pulp
4 oz (100 g) tomato purée
1 tbsp freshly grated ginger
2 curry leaves
3 tbsp garam masala
2 tbsp sesame seeds
3 pints (1 1/2 l) poultry stock
1 lb 5 oz (600 g) frozen peas
salt, pepper, mustard powder
7 oz (200 g) cream
1 bunch of coriander, to garnish

Preparation time: approx. 50 minutes

483 cal/2027 kJ

■ How to do it:

Peel the onions and cut into rings and peel cloves of garlic and chop up finely. Wash the chilli peppers and cut in half, remove seeds and chop into strips. Heat up the ghee, add onions and garlic and then the chillies and fry gently for 5 minutes. Put the tamarind in water and allow to steep for 12 minutes. Press out the juice through a sieve and add the tomato purée, ginger, crushed curry leaves and garam masala. Now add the stock, thawed peas, and onion mix. Season to taste with salt, pepper and mustard powder and then cook on a low heat for 10 minutes. Finally liquidise with a hand-blender and stir in cream. Decorate with the coriander leaves and serve.

1 Cut the onions into rings.

2 Cut the chilli peppers into strips.

3 Add the peas.

4 Liquidise the soup with a hand-blender.

CUCUMBER RAITA

Serves 4

1 salad cucumber
7 oz (200 g) cream
7 oz (200 g) yoghurt
4 tbsp double cream
1/2 bunch fresh coriander
1/2 bunch fresh mint
2 green chilli peppers
1 red chilli pepper
salt
pepper
1 tbsp each: cumin, mustard,
coriander and black cumin
seeds
fresh coriander and mint,
to garnish

Preparation time: approx. 35 minutes
368 cal/1544 kJ

■ How to do it:

Wash, dry and cut ends off the cucumber and chop into cubes. Mix
together the cream, yoghurt and
double cream and add to the cucumber. Wash and dry the herbs
and chop up finely and also add to
the cucumber mix. Wash the chilli
peppers and cut in half, remove
seeds and chop into strips and add
to mix. Season to taste with salt and
pepper and then allow it to cool for
20 minutes. While waiting roast the

seeds in a pan until you can detect
their aroma and they have all burst,
sprinkle over the raita. Garnish with
the mint and coriander and serve.

COCONUT FISH SOUP

Serves 4

9 oz (250 g) fresh coconut flesh

4 potatoes

4 oz (100 g) red lentils

3 pints (1 1/2 l) fish stock

1 tsp turmeric powder

1 tbsp freshly ground ginger

1 bunch spring onions

4 cloves of garlic

4 tbsp sunflower oil

1 lb 5 oz (600 g) saltwater
fish fillet

3 tbsp tamarind juice

4 tbsp garam masala

4 fl oz (100 ml) coconut milk

3 tbsp coconut cream

salt

pepper

Preparation time: approx. 45 minutes

528 cal/2216 kJ

■ How to do it:

Chop the coconut flesh into cubes. Peel the potatoes and chop into small pieces. Add together with the coconut pieces and lentils to the fish stock and cook at a low heat for approximately 20 minutes. Add the turmeric and ginger and then liquidise everything with a hand-blender. Trim, wash and chop the spring onions into rings. Peel the cloves of garlic and chop up finely. Heat the oil and gently fry the garlic and onions. Wash and dry the fish, cut into cubes and add to the pan. Pour in the tamarind juice and garam masala, as well as the coconut milk and cream. Finally pour over with the coconut-lentil purée, season with salt and pepper and serve.

Coconut

Coconut is a very nutritional food that is valued in India. It is rich in minerals, vitamins and fat. Growing in India they are almost exclusively used fresh, which of course is much tastier than the dried variety.

Tamarind

Tamarinds are also known as Indian dates and are derived from the fleshy fruit of a tropical plant. Brownish-black in colour with a taste reminiscent of cooking plums.

LENTIL RAITA

Serves 4

1 lb 5 oz (600 g) green lentils
17–18 fl oz (500 ml) each:
lamb and vegetable stock
salt
4 red chilli peppers
3 curry leaves
3 tbsp curry powder
chickpea flour to thicken
oil for deep frying
14 oz (400 g) natural yoghurt
14 oz (400 g) cream
4 oz (100 g) double cream
1/2–1 tsp each: ground cumin,
fennel and mustard powder

Preparation time: approx. 45 minutes

685 cal/2877 kJ

■ How to do it:

Add lentils to the stock mix and bring to the boil. Wash the chilli peppers and cut in half, remove seeds and chop into strips. Add together with the curry leaves and cook everything on a low heat for approximately 20 minutes. Then stir in the curry powder and liquidise with a hand-blender. If the lentil purée has too thin a consistency, then add chick-pea flour and stir in to thicken it up. Roll the mixture into small balls with wet hands and deep fry in oil until golden yellow. Mix together the yo-ghurt, cream and double cream and add the fennel, cumin and mustard powder to taste. Serve the lentil balls together with the raita dip.

Fennel

Fennel's sweet taste is familiar to us as tea, sweets or for Christmas baking. A healthy vegetable, it can be found in many Indian dishes. Fennel seeds are also well regarded particularly for their use in improving digestion.

1 Stir in the curry powder.

2 Form balls out of mixture using wet hands.

3 Deep fry small lentil balls in hot oil.

4 Season the yoghurt dip to taste.

LAMB-MUNG BEAN BROTH

VARIATION

Instead of making broth out of bones, use vegetables and stewing meat. The meat can be later cut into strips and added to the soup.

Serves 4

2 lb 3 oz (1 kg) lamb bones
1 lb 2 oz (500 g) poultry scraps
10 shallots
5 cloves of garlic
4 tbsp peanut oil
6 carrots
2 cinnamon sticks
12 cloves
12 pimento seeds
1 tsp each: white and black peppercorns
2 bay leaves
1 tsp salt
10–11 oz (300 g) shoulder of lamb
9 oz (250 g) mung beans
2 tbsp garam masala
salt
pepper
1 bunch of coriander

Preparation time: approx. 40 minutes
(excluding stewing time)
625 cal/2625 kJ

■ How to do it:

Chop the bones and poultry scraps into pieces. Peel the shallots and cut into cubes. Peel the cloves of garlic and chop into pieces. Add all these ingredients to some heated oil and fry a little then add 2 pints 13 fl oz (1 1/2 l) water. Peel and chop the carrots and then add together with the cinnamon sticks, cloves, pimento, pepper, bay leaves and salt to the water and then stew on a very low heat for 3 hours. When ready pour the stock through a sieve. Chop the meat into cubes and add to the stock. Cook on a low heat for 20 minutes. Wash and dry the mung beans and add to soup for the last 5 minutes of cooking. Season with garam masala, salt and pepper. Wash and dry the coriander pick off some leaves and use to garnish. The soup is now ready to serve.

CHILLED VEGETABLE-YOGHURT SOUP

Serves 4

14 oz (400 g) each: cauliflower
and broccoli
1 1/2 pint (1 l) vegetable stock
9 fl oz (250 ml) poultry stock
1 tsp ground turmeric
3 tbsp lemon juice
10–11 oz (300 g) natural
yoghurt
1 tsp each: cumin, coriander,
and pimento powder
1/2 salad cucumber
3 curry leaves
2 red chilli peppers
4 tsp finely chopped walnuts,
to garnish

Preparation time: approx. 30 minutes
(excluding cooling time)
194 cal/813 kJ

■ How to do it:

Trim the cauliflower and broccoli,
wash and break into florets. Add to
the vegetable and poultry stock and
cook for 10 minutes. Add the turmeric and lemon juice. Allow it to
cool slightly and then liquidise with
a hand-blender. Stir in the yoghurt
and season with the cumin, coriander and pimento powder. Cut the
cucumber into cubes and add, then
sprinkle with crushed curry leaves
and finely chopped chilli peppers.
Allow everything to cool for another
10 minutes. Roast the walnuts in a
pan without oil. Sprinkle over the
soup, garnish with mint and serve.

AROMATIC VEG-ETARIAN DISHES

Rice, Vegetables and Dals

Rice plays a very central role in every Indian meal. A particular favourite is aromatic basmati rice that these days is very well known all over the world and considered by many to be a delicacy. As well as rice, a rich variety of vegetables and pulses or "dals" in India are also highly rated ingredients. This is particularly the case amongst vegetarians, who in fact make up the majority in India. The many combinations of rice, vegetables, herbs and spices are proof enough that vegetarian cuisine in India is not only healthy and balanced but also very diverse and quite simply delicious.

Basmati rice

India's most famous rice is mostly grown on the slopes of the Himalayas. The thin, slightly curved grains have a unique delicate taste.

Courgette

Courgettes can be light green, yellow or white. They belong to the pumpkin family of plants and have a somewhat nutty taste that blends very well with most seasonings. The smaller courgettes (approx. 7 oz/200 g) are the tastiest.

Okras

Okras have a characteristic six-sided sprout that usually has a light green or yellow colour. Their taste is mild and herby and they are very rich in vitamins and low in calories.

Cottage cheese

This fresh, textured, slightly dry cheese is already well established in European cuisine. It is very similar to the Indian home-made quark known as "paneer" that is used in many dishes. Cottage cheese however serves as a good substitute for this.

VEGETABLE BIRYANI

Serves 4

1 lb (450 g) basmati rice
4 Spanish onions
3 cloves of garlic
4 tbsp ghee or sunflower oil
1 tbsp each: ground cloves, cardamom and turmeric
1 tbsp garam masala
4 oz (100 g) each: finely chopped carrots, cauliflower, courgettes and okras
2 1/2 pints (1 1/2 l) vegetable stock
salt
cayenne pepper
4 oz (100 g) cottage cheese
4 oz (100 g) sultanas
5 oz (125 g) each: chopped almonds and cashews
fried onions, to garnish

Preparation time: approx. 40 minutes
923 cal/3875 kJ

■ How to do it:

Put the rice in a sieve and wash it until the draining water becomes clear. Peel onions and chop up finely. Peel the garlic and chop up finely. Melt the ghee in a pan and gently fry onions and garlic. Add the rice and season with the ground cloves, cardamom and turmeric and then the garam masala. Add the rice and then pour the vegetable stock over everything. Add salt and pepper to taste. Cook on a low heat for approximately 18 minutes. Fold in the cottage cheese, nuts and sultanas when the rice has absorbed all the water. Leave to stand for 5 minutes. Garnish with lightly fried onions and serve.

1 Fry the onions and garlic in ghee.

2 Add the rice.

3 Pour the vegetable stock over all the ingredients.

4 Fold in the cottage cheese when the rice has absorbed all its water.

SPICY WHITE CABBAGE

Serves 4

3 Spanish onions
6 cloves of garlic
1 lb 5 oz (600 g) white cabbage
9 oz (250 g) green peas
9 oz (250 g) carrots
7 oz (200 g) potatoes
9 oz (250 g) tomatoes
3 tbsp ghee or olive oil
1 tsp white cumin seeds
1 tbsp ground turmeric
2 tsp mango powder
3 green chilli peppers
1 tbsp freshly grated ginger
1 tbsp garam masala
1/2 bunch of coriander
3 tbsp butter, melted

Preparation time: approx. 30 minutes
255 cal/1071 kJ

■ How to do it:

Peel the onions and cut into cubes. Peel the cloves of garlic and chop up finely. Clean and rinse white cabbage and cut into strips. Wash the peas and put to one side. Peel carrots and chop into thin strips. Peel potatoes and cut into small cubes. Wash tomatoes and cut into small wedges. Melt the ghee in a pan and gently fry the onions and garlic. Add the vegetables and fry for 8 minutes. Season using the cumin seeds, ground turmeric and mango powder. Wash the chilli peppers and cut in half, remove seeds, chop up finely and add to the vegetables. Season with the ginger and garam masala. Wash and dry coriander and pluck off the leaves. Serve the hot vegetables on plates, garnished with melted butter and coriander leaves.

SAFFRON RICE

Serves 4

1 tbsp saffron threads
6 shallots
4 tbsp lard
14 oz (400 g) basmati rice
1 tsp cloves
1 pinch of ground cardamom
1 cinnamon stick
1/2 tsp freshly grated nutmeg
salt
pepper

Preparation time: approx. 40 minutes
450 cal/1890 kJ

■ **How to do it:**

Pour 1 pint 15 fl oz (1 l) hot water over the dried saffron threads and soak for 20 minutes. While waiting peel the shallots and cut into cubes. Melt the lard in a pan and gently fry the shallots. Add washed rice and continue to fry. Pour 1 pint 2 fl oz (600 ml) water onto the rice, etc and then add the cloves, cardamom, cinnamon, and nutmeg. Add saffron threads including liquid and simmer everything for about 18 minutes or until the rice is firm but tender. Add salt and pepper to taste. Prepare in bowls and serve.

Saffron

Saffron is the most expensive spice in the world, and quite rightly so. The bright orange blossom threads (stigmas) are taken from the flowers of a type of crocus plant and they must be handpicked. Saffron is spicy and slightly bitter and is used particularly for its intense yellow colour.

Nutmeg

Nutmeg is a very popular spice and mostly used in vegetable dishes, soups and sauces. It tastes its best when freshly grated.

FINE CHICKPEAS

Serves 4

10–11 oz (300 g) chickpeas
9 fl oz (250 ml) vegetable stock
8 shallots
2 each: green and red chilli peppers
4 tbsp sunflower oil
2 tbsp freshly grated ginger
1 tsp ground turmeric
1 tbsp cayenne pepper
2 tbsp garam masala
5 oz (120 g) tinned peeled tomatoes
2 tbsp lemon juice
1 Spanish onion
3 tbsp olive oil
salt

Preparation time: approx. 1 hour 10 minutes
(excluding soaking time)
265 cal/1113 kJ

Sunflower oil

Sunflower (like olive) is one of the better known of the oils. It has a mildly nutty and light taste, and is rich in essential unsaturated fats and vitamin E.

■ **How to do it:**

Wash and drain the chickpeas, removing any bad ones. Leave overnight to soak in water. On the following day add the vegetable stock to the rest of the water and cook the chickpeas on a low heat for approximately 1 hour. They are ready when tender but still firm. While waiting peel the shallots and cut into cubes. Wash the chilli peppers, cut in half, remove seeds and chop into strips. Heat up the oil in a pan, add shallots and chilli peppers and fry gently. Season everything with the ginger, turmeric, cayenne pepper and garam masala. Chop up tomatoes and add to the ingredients. Stir in the lemon juice and cook for 3 minutes. Drain off the chickpea stock leaving about 18 fl oz (1/2 l) and add the chickpeas and stock to the rest of the ingredients folding them in gently. Cook for a further 3 minutes. Peel the onions and cut into thin rings, add them to some heated oil and fry gently. Add salt. Divide chickpeas into portions, garnish with onions and serve with rice or bread.

1 Cut chilli peppers into strips.

2 Add chopped tomatoes.

3 Fold in chickpeas together with remaining liquid.

4 Gently fry thin onion rings.

PULAO WITH NUTS

VARIATION

Instead of using sultanas try stirring in 7 oz (200 g) red kidney beans and half a bunch of coriander. Spice everything up with a little chilli powder.

Serves 4

8 green cardamom pods
8 cloves
1/2 tbsp each: black and white peppercorns
1 cinnamon stick
(approx. 2 inches/5 cm)
3 tbsp ghee or lard
1/2 ground saffron
12 oz (350 g) Patna rice
13 fl oz (375 ml) vegetable stock
salt
pepper
2 tsp orange peel aroma
2 tbsp sultanas
3 tbsp chopped walnuts

Preparation time: approx. 35 minutes
493 cal/2069 kJ

■ How to do it:

Crack open cardamom pods, cloves, pepper and cinnamon using a mortar. Melt the ghee in a pan and then add the spices, gently frying them. Introduce rice and ground saffron. After about 3 minutes, when the rice grains turn glassy, pour the vegetable stock over everything. Season with the salt, pepper and orange peel aroma, then allow to simmer for 20 minutes or until the liquid has been cooked away. Add the sultanas and gently loosen up the rice with a fork. Gently roast the walnuts in a pan without using any oil, sprinkle over rice and serve.

ALOO CAKES

Serves 4

1 lb 5 oz (600 g) cooking
potatoes (salted)
7 oz (200 g) leaf spinach
9 oz (250 g) cherry tomatoes
4 Spanish onions
4 tbsp sunflower oil
1 tbsp freshly grated ginger
2 tsp mustard powder
1 tsp ground turmeric
2 tsp chilli powder
3 tbsp lemon juice
milk
1 bunch of coriander
6 tbsp grated cashew nuts
oil, for frying

Preparation time: approx. 45 minutes
450 cal/1890 kJ

■ How to do it:

Cook the potatoes unpeeled in slightly salted water for approximately 20 minutes. While waiting trim, wash and dry the spinach leaves. Wash the tomatoes and cut into wedges. Peel the onions and chop into small cubes. Heat the oil in a pan, add spinach, onions and tomatoes and fry gently. Season with the mustard, turmeric and chilli powder. Stir in the lemon juice. Drain the potatoes, peel and together with some milk and salt partially mash them into a rough consistency. Wash and dry the coriander leaves and chop up finely. Add the coriander and potatoes to the spinach and allow some time to cool. With wetted hands form small flat cakes out of the mixture, rolling them over the grated nuts to finish. Heat the oil in a pan and fry cakes on both sides until golden brown. Serve with chutney or pickles.

Aniseed mushrooms

Aniseed mushrooms have a fine flavour that goes extremely well with Indian dishes. In Europe they are mostly associated with French cuisine.

Lemon grass

This herb has a strong lemon type aroma and is very popular as a fresh ingredient in Indian cooking, particularly in dishes with Persian origins. You will usually find it freshly chopped in well-stocked supermarkets.

Patna rice

This rice takes its name from the north Indian city situated on the banks of the Ganges. Patna rice has long thin rounded grains and is of a high quality.

Thai-soi

Thai-soi is also known as chopping garlic and therefore a practical herb indeed. The taste lies somewhere between garlic and chives and is ideal for those who like to enjoy garlic but in a milder form.

STUFFED PEPPERS

Serves 4

8 small peppers
1 Spanish onion
5 tbsp sunflower oil
2 tbsp ground turmeric
1 tbsp ground cumin
1/2 tbsp chilli powder
1 lb 5 oz (600 g) aniseed mushrooms
1/2 bunch thai-soi
1 tsp freshly chopped lemon grass
6 tbsp Patna rice
10–11 oz (300 g) tinned peeled tomatoes
salt

Preparation time: approx. 50 minutes
253 cal/1061 kJ

■ How to do it:

Wash the bell peppers, cut in half and remove stalk, seeds and inner white flesh. Peel onion and chop into cubes. Heat up the oil in a pan and gently fry onions until they become glassy. Stir in the ground turmeric, cumin powder and chilli powder. Wash and dry the mushrooms cut into small pieces and add to the spices. Wash and dry the thai-soi and chop into small rings and stir in together with the lemon grass. Add rice and gently fry until the grains become glassy. Pour half of the tinned peeled tomatoes together with some juice and cook on a low heat for 12 minutes. Allow mixture to cool down a little and then stuff into the insides of the peppers. Take the rest of the tomatoes and fry gently in a pan with a sprinkling of salt. Lay stuffed peppers on top of sauce and heat gently for 8 minutes. Serve together with the puréed tomatoes and some bread.

1 Cut the peppers in half.

2 Gently fry and season the onion.

3 Chop the thai-soi into little rings.

4 Pour half of tinned peeled tomatoes with juice over ingredients.

LENTIL MADRAS

Serves 4

6 tbsp sunflower oil
8 cloves
8 green cardamom pods
2 cinnamon sticks
(approx. 3/4 inch/2 cm)
3 red onions
3 cloves of garlic
2 red chilli peppers
1 green chilli pepper
2 tbsp freshly grated ginger
1 tbsp garam masala
12 oz (350 g) puy lentils
1 pint 2 fl oz (600 ml) vegetable stock
5 tbsp lemon juice
5 tbsp natural yoghurt
1 tbsp double cream
1/2 bunch of coriander
fresh coriander leaves, to garnish

Preparation time: approx. 30 minutes
375 cal/1575 kJ

■ **How to do it:**

Heat up the oil in a pan and gently fry the cloves, cardamom and cinnamon. Peel the onions and cut into cubes. Peel the cloves of garlic and crush. Wash the chilli peppers and cut in half, remove seeds and chop into strips. Add these to the pan and continue to fry, seasoning with the ginger and garam masala. Add the lentils and vegetable stock and cook on a low heat for 18 minutes. Once everything is cooked stir in the lemon juice, yoghurt and double cream. Wash and dry the fresh coriander, chop up finely and stir in as well. Serve garnished with the coriander leaves.

BAKED COLOURED RICE

Serves 4

14oz (400 g) basmati rice
1 pint 7 fl oz (750 ml) vegetable stock
1 tbsp salt, 1 tbsp ground turmeric
3 tsp butter
10–11 oz (300 g) each: horse radish, carrots, and turnip
10–11 oz (300 g) tomatoes
4 shallots, 4 cloves of garlic
5 tbsp lard
2 tbsp freshly grated ginger
1 tbsp chilli powder
1/2 tbsp each: ground cumin and coriander
butter, to grease dish
chopped mint, to garnish

Preparation time: approx. 50 minutes
643 cal/2699 kJ

■ How to do it:

Put the rice in a sieve and wash until the water draining off it is clear.

Heat up the vegetable stock, and then add the ground turmeric, salt and rice. Cook for at least 6 minutes, then drain away excess liquid and allow the rice to drip dry. Mix the rice together with the butter in a large bowl. Peel the turnip and cut into slices. Wash the tomatoes, pierce skin and put briefly in boiling water, then remove, peel and chop into cubes. Peel the shallots and cut into cubes. Peel the garlic and crush. Heat up lard and gently fry the turnip, tomatoes, shallots and garlic. Season everything with the ginger, chilli, cumin and coriander. Preheat the oven to gas mark 3–4, 338 °F (170 °C). Grease a casserole dish and fill the bottom with half of the vegetable mixture. Add the rice and then layer the rest of the vegetables on top. Cover the dish with aluminium foil and place on the middle shelf of the oven and bake for approx. 20 minutes. Serve garnished with fresh mint.

Horse radish

This white radish, popular in Europe, is also often used in Indian cooking, either in pickles or sautéed.

Turnip

This is a very diverse root vegetable that grows all over the world and comes in different sizes, colours and tastes. The white May turnip has a very mild taste.

SPICY CAULIFLOWER

Serves 4

1 large cauliflower
salt
2 each: red, yellow, and green peppers
4 shallots
4 cloves of garlic
1 tbsp freshly grated ginger
2 tbsp garam masala
4 tbsp tomato purée
1 tbsp chilli powder
4 tbsp lard
4 oz (100 g) natural yoghurt
4 tbsp double cream
6 tbsp pine nuts
chervil, to garnish

Preparation time: approx. 25 minutes
278 cal/1166 kJ

■ How to do it:

Trim and wash the cauliflower, then break it off into florets. Blanch in slightly salted water for approximately 5 minutes. Remove and drain. Wash the bell peppers and cut in half, remove seeds and chop into cubes. Peel the shallots and garlic and chop finely. Add all of these ingredients, apart from the cauliflower, to a bowl and mix together with the ginger, garam masala, tomato purée and the chilli powder. Heat up the lard and gently fry the mixture for 6 minutes. Add the cauliflower and fry together for about 3 minutes. Stir in the yoghurt and double cream. Gently roast the pine nuts in a pan without using oil and then sprinkle on top of the cauliflower mix. Garnish with chervil and serve.

Pine nuts

Pine nuts are actually the seeds out of pinecones. The thin yellow-white kernels are smooth and soft and taste similar to almonds. Like almonds they also have a very high content of protein, fat, carbohydrates and minerals

1 Break off small florets from the cauliflower.

2 Peel the shallots and garlic and chop up finely.

3 Gently fry the mixture in melted lard.

4 Stir in the yoghurt and double cream.

AUBERGINES WITH YOGHURT SAUCE

VARIATION

Replace half of the aubergines with potatoes and add more garlic. This will add about 8 minutes to the cooking time.

Serves 4

1 1/2 oz (850 g) aubergines
3 tbsp lemon juice
4 red onions
3 cloves of garlic
5 tbsp lard
2 tbsp freshly grated ginger
4 green chilli peppers
3 tbsp curry powder
1 tbsp ground coriander
7 fl oz (200 ml) vegetable stock
3 tbsp freshly chopped basil
4 oz (100 g) natural yoghurt
2 tbsp cream

Preparation time: approx. 25 minutes

383 cal/1607 kJ

■ How to do it:

Wash the aubergines, chop off the stalks and cut into slices. Sprinkle the lemon juice on top of the slices. Peel the onions and garlic, chop up finely. Heat up lard in a pan and gently fry the aubergines, garlic and onions. Season with the ginger. Wash the chilli peppers and cut in half, remove seeds and chop up finely and add together with the curry powder and ground coriander. After approximately 3 minutes pour the vegetable stock over everything and leave it to cook for another 5 minutes. Stir together the basil, yoghurt and cream in a bowl, and warm up gently. Dress the aubergines and serve.

EKURI – INDIAN SCRAMBLED EGGS

Serves 4

5 shallots
2 each: green and red chilli
peppers
1 tsp each: ground cardamom,
cumin and black cumin
1 tsp ground turmeric
5 tbsp butter
5 tbsp tomato purée
10 eggs
5–6 fl oz (150 ml) mineral
water
3 tbsp freshly chopped green
coriander

Preparation time: approx. 20 minutes
300 cal/1260 kJ

■ How to do it:

Peel the shallots and chop up finely.
Wash the chilli peppers and cut in
half, remove seeds and chop into
strips. Season the shallots and chillies
with the ground cardamom, cumin,
black cumin and turmeric. Melt the
butter in a pan and fry everything for
4 minutes. Whisk the eggs together
with the mineral water and fold the
green coriander into the mixture.
Add this to the spices and stir until
the mixture begins to stiffen up.
Prepare on a plate and serve. Lentil
wafers go very well with this dish.

A SUCCESS STORY

Currys and Vindaloos

Curry is India's national dish and most famous export product. Its popularity has helped to establish a name for itself the world over and therefore needs little introduction. Curry and Vindaloo recipes exist in an infinite variety that is continuously being refined and embellished. A curry is always strong in flavour but not necessarily hot. The amount of chilli peppers used is decisive to the dishes spiciness, and this starts at mild and can go up to "hotter than hot". Vindaloos on the other hand are situated more around the top of scale in terms of spiciness and at their strongest they are simply "hotter than hell".

Cardamom

Cardamom is one of the most used herbs in Indian cooking. It has a mildly spicy flavour and is best purchased in the form of light green pods (with the seed inside). These can either be used whole or cracked and/or ground.

Cloves

Cloves are the dried buds of the clove tree, which has many similarities with myrtle. Their strong peppery taste is very unique but used correctly they are suitable for many dishes. They are especially favoured for meat or vegetable recipes and often used for sweets.

Cumin

Cumin has a fiery spiciness and a slightly bitter taste. It is one of the main ingredients for the famous Indian spice blends such as curry and garam masala.

Bay leaves

The evergreen bay tree produces a tough, shiny dark green leaf. They are first split and then cooked in a sauce whole. The leaves are not eaten however, but are usually removed before serving.

KASHMIR CURRY

Serves 4

2 lb 3 oz (1 kg) shoulder of lamb
5–6 oz (150 g) chickpea flour
4 tbsp garam masala
1 tsp cayenne pepper
salt
7 oz (200 g) yoghurt
4 tbsp sunflower oil
1 cinnamon stick
(approx. 2 inches/5 cm)
10 green cardamom pods
3 bay leaves
2 tbsp freshly grated ginger
18 fl oz (500 ml) lamb stock
fresh coriander leaves,
to garnish

Preparation time: approx. 40 minutes
660 cal/2772 kJ

■ How to do it:

Wash and dry the meat and cut into cubes and then mince up finely. Mix the minced meat with the flour, garam masala, pepper and salt, and half of the yoghurt and then knead it all together. With wet hands divide the mass into 20 portions and then roll each one into small fat sausage shapes. Heat up the oil and gently fry the cinnamon, cardamom, bay leaves and cloves for 2 minutes. Add the meat rolls and fry for a further 4 minutes. Sprinkle the ginger over the rolls and then pour in the rest of the yoghurt and the lamb stock. Turn down the heat and simmer for approximately 15 minutes. Wash and dry the coriander, and pluck off the leaves. Use to garnish the rolls and serve with rice or bread.

1 Chop the meat into cubes.

2 Knead half of the yoghurt into the meat mass.

3 Roll the meat mass into shape.

4 Add the meat rolls to the spices and fry.

VEGETABLE CURRY

Serves 4

**9 oz (250 g) each: okras, green
beans, carrots and potatoes**
4 red onions
4 tbsp lard
2 tbsp fennel seeds
2 tbsp chilli powder
1 tbsp ground coriander
3 tbsp curry powder
2 tbsp freshly grated ginger
**14 fl oz (400 ml) vegetable
stock**
**9 oz (250 g) tinned peeled
tomatoes**
6 assorted chilli peppers
cornflour, to thicken

Preparation time: approx. 45 minutes
315 cal/1323 kJ

■ How to do it:

Wash the okras and chop off the
stalks. Trim, wash and dry the beans.
Peel the carrots and cut into thin
strips. Peel and wash the potatoes
and also cut into thin strips. Peel the
onions and dice. Melt the lard in a
pan and add the onions, gently frying them. Add the fennel seeds and
continue to fry for about 2 minutes.
Now add all the vegetables and
season with the spices. Pour the
vegetable stock and the tomatoes

onto the vegetables. Wash the chilli
peppers and cut in half, remove
seeds, chop into strips and add
to the sauce. Cook everything for
about 20 minutes and thicken with
cornflour if necessary. Serve with
saffron rice.

DUCK VINDALOO

Serves 4

3 green cardamom pods
3 cloves
1 cinnamon stick
(approx. 1/2 inch/1 cm)
2 curry leaves
1/2 tsp cumin seeds
1/2 tsp mustard seeds
1/2 tsp each: paprika powder
and dried lemon grass
2 red onions
2 cloves of garlic
1 green chilli pepper
2 red chilli peppers
2 tbsp sunflower oil
1 tbsp freshly grated ginger
1 tbsp tomato purée
1 tsp sherry vinegar
13/4 lb (800 g) duck breast
with skin
1 Spanish onion
4 oz (100 g) thai-soi
4 tbsp lard
7 fl oz (200 ml) vegetable stock

Preparation time: approx. 45 minutes

315 cal/1323 kJ

■ How to do it:

Roast the cardamom, cloves, cinnamon and curry in a pan without oil. Add the cumin, mustard, paprika and lemon grass and roast for a further 3 minutes. Leave to cool and then grind finely. Peel the red onions and garlic and chop up finely. Wash the chilli peppers and cut in half, remove seeds and chop up finely. Heat up the oil in the pan and gently fry the onions and garlic together with the chillies and ginger. Add the tomato purée and vinegar and then stir in the spices and continue to fry gently. While cooking press the mixture down with a fork to make into a paste. Put the ready paste to one side. Peel the onion and chop up finely. Wash and dry thai-soi and cut into small rings. Heat up lard and gently fry onion and thai-soi. Add meat and fry for about another 4 minutes. Add vindaloo paste and the vegetable stock. Cook everything for another 25 minutes on a low heat. Serve on a large plate.

Duck breast

You can buy duck breast with or without it's skin. For stewing or frying it is better to take with skin, thereby keeping it tender and juicy.

Lard

Lard is ideal for frying and deep fat frying, because you can heat it up to a high temperature without it burning. During manufacture the protein and water is removed from the butter leaving lard, which holds the fat content and remaining minerals.

CHICKEN CURRY

Serves 4

1 poulard
4 shallots
2 carrots
3 cloves of garlic
2 stalks of celery
4 tbsp lard
2 tbsp freshly grated ginger
2 tbsp coriander seeds
1 tbsp pimento seeds
2 bay leaves
2 tbsp cloves
1 tbsp cumin seeds
1 tbsp black pepper corns
2 tbsp green cardamom pods
4 Spanish onions
4 oz (100 g) thai-soi
5 green chilli peppers
4 tbsp ghee or lard
1 tbsp each: ground turmeric,
coriander and cumin
2 tbsp lemon juice
2 bunches of fresh coriander
celery leaves, to garnish

Preparation time: approx. 35 minutes
(excluding marinating time)
475 cal/1995 kJ

■ How to do it:

Wash and dry the poulard and put it in a pot and cover with little over 3 pints (2 l) of water. Peel the shallots, carrots and garlic and cut into pieces. Remove the leaves from the celery and cut the stalks into small pieces. Melt the lard in a pan and add the vegetables to it, frying them gently. Add the ginger and all the spices including the cardamom to the meat and cook on a low heat for about an hour. Once ready remove the meat, bone it and put it to one side. Pour the stock through a sieve. Peel the onions and cut into cubes. Wash and dry the thai-soi and cut into little rings. Wash the chilli peppers and cut in half, remove the seeds and chop up finely. Heat the ghee and gently fry the thai-soi and onions. Add the meat and chillies and season with the ground turmeric, coriander, and cumin. Pour over 14 fl oz (400 ml) of the stock and the lemon juice and cook for a further 4 minutes. Wash and dry coriander, chop up finely and stir into the sauce shortly before serving. Garnish with the celery leaves.

Garlic

Garlic is one of the strongest and healthiest types of seasoning that can be used in a number of ways for cooking. If you find its taste too strong, however try using garlic that has been soaked in olive oil.

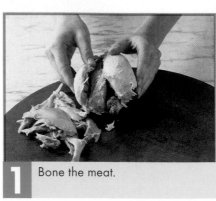

1 Bone the meat.

2 Gently fry the onions and thai-soi in some ghee.

3 Add the chillies and meat.

4 Pour 14 fl oz (400 ml) of the stock over meat and leave to cook.

PRAWN VINDALOO

VARIATION

Instead of using king prawns try mackerel and eel fillets. Use more garlic when cooking and serve on a bed of deep fried potato slices.

Serves 4

3 lb 5 oz (1,5 kg) king prawns (unpeeled)
3 tbsp vinegar
6 cloves of garlic
8 shallots
2 each: red and green chilli peppers
4 tbsp ghee or lard
3 tbsp vindaloo paste (ready made or see page 77)
1 tbsp chilli powder
6 preserved tomatoes
4 tbsp lobster stock
1/2 bunch of basil, to garnish

Preparation time: approx. 30 minutes
430 cal/1806 kJ

■ **How to do it:**

Wash and dry the king prawns. Peel them carefully by breaking and pulling off the shell and separating the innards from the meat. Sprinkle some vinegar over the prawns. Peel the garlic and chop up finely. Peel the shallots and chop into cubes. Wash the chilli peppers and cut in half, remove the seeds and chop up finely. Melt the ghee in a pan and gently fry the shallots, garlic and chilli peppers. Add the prawns and season with the vindaloo paste and chilli powder. Wash the tomatoes, cut into thin wedges and add. Stir in the lobster stock. Fry everything for at least 6 minutes. Wash and dry the basil cut into strips and use to garnish the vindaloo. Serve with rice or bread.

LENTIL CURRY WITH MUSHROOMS

Serves 4

9 oz (250 g) chanterelle mushrooms
2 tbsp lemon juice
2 tbsp garam masala
9 oz (250 g) Indian lentils
1 pint 2 fl oz (600 ml) vegetable stock
10 cloves of garlic
4 shallots
4 green chilli peppers
4 tbsp lard
4 tbsp curry powder
1 tbsp ground turmeric
2 tbsp freshly grated ginger
4 tbsp tomato purée

Preparation time: approx. 45 minutes
365 cal/1533 kJ

■ How to do it:

Trim and wash the mushrooms and sprinkle with lemon juice and then with the garam masala. Wash the lentils and cook in the vegetable stock for about 20 minutes. When ready drain through a sieve, collecting the stock to use later and placing the lentils to one side. Peel the garlic and press. Peel the shallots and cut into cubes. Wash the chilli peppers and cut in half, remove seeds and chop up finely. Melt the lard in a pan and gently fry the garlic. Add the mushrooms, shallots and chillies and season with the curry powder, ground turmeric and ginger. Stir in the tomato purée and cook everything for 3 minutes. Add 7 fl oz (200 ml) of the vegetable stock and cook for a further 3 minutes. Finally stir in the lentils, dish into small bowls and serve together with rice.

Fruit vinegar

You can use many different types of vinegar to prepare the vindaloo paste, but particularly good is fruit vinegar, which is made out of over-fermented fruit wine. Apple vinegar gives a very special taste.

Wine vinegar

Made from red or white grape wine, this will give the vindaloo paste a certain fruity, soft taste.

Sherry vinegar

This offers a more richer flavour than the wine vinegar and as the name suggests, leaves a definite sherry aftertaste.

Malt vinegar

Malt vinegar is a darker or lighter form of wine vinegar and has a strong aroma.

POULTRY VINDALOO

Serves 4

3 lb 5 oz (1,5 kg) turkey breast fillet
6 tbsp vindaloo paste (ready made or see page 77)
2 tsp salt
1 tbsp mustard powder
4 bay leaves, 4 red onions
4 tbsp olive oil
1 tbsp ground cardamom
1 tbsp ground turmeric
1 tbsp chilli powder
2 freshly grated ginger
10 cloves of garlic
4 tbsp tomato puree
4 tbsp lemon juice
9 fl oz (250 ml) vegetable stock
1 tbsp beetroot juice
4 coconut flakes

Preparation time: approx. 40 minutes
(excluding marinating time)
462 cal/1942 kJ

■ **How to do it:**

Wash and dry the meat and prick the flesh several times with a knife. Stir salt and mustard powder into the paste and then brush the mixture onto the meat, covering it as much as possible. Place the bay leaves on top and wrap in aluminium foil. Leave to cure for 3 hours. When ready cut into cubes. Peel the onions and cut into cubes. Heat up the oil and fry the onions and meat together. Season everything with the ground cardamom, turmeric, chilli powder and ginger. Peel the garlic and press over the meat. Stir in the tomato purée and fry for a further 6 minutes. Mix the lemon juice, stock and beetroot juice together and pour over the meat. Cook for a further 10 minutes. Roast the coconut flakes in a pan without using any oil, sprinkle over the meat and serve.

1 Stir the salt and mustard powder into the paste.

2 Brush the paste mix onto the meat.

3 Top with the bay leaves and wrap in aluminium foil.

4 Fry the chopped meat with the onions.

AUBERGINE AND CAULIFLOWER CURRY

Serves 4

8 eggs
4 cloves of garlic
8 shallots
6 tbsp lard
3 tbsp curry powder
4 oz (100 g) tinned peeled
tomatoes
10–11 oz (300 g) each:
aubergine and cauliflower
14 fl oz (400 ml) vegetable stock
3 tbsp garam masala
1 tbsp lemon juice
7 oz (200 g) yoghurt
3 tbsp cream
1/2 bunch of fresh coriander

Preparation time: approx. 25 minutes
482 cal/2026 kJ

■ **How to do it:**

Medium boil the eggs (about 6 minutes). Rinse under cold water, peel off their shell and cut into small wedges. Peel the garlic and chop up finely. Peel the shallots and chop into cubes. Melt lard in a pan and gently fry the garlic and shallots. Season with curry powder and add the tomatoes together with their juices. Wash the cauliflower and

break off into small florets. Wash the aubergines and cut into slices. Add to the shallots and fry briefly. Then pour the vegetable stock onto everything. Season the sauce with the lemon juice and garam masala. After cooking for about 6 minutes stir in the yoghurt and cream. Wash and dry the coriander, pluck off leaves and also stir into sauce. Prepare on a plate decorated with the egg wedges and serve with bread.

LAMB VINDALOO

Serves 4

12 oz (350 g) potatoes
salt
2 1/4 lb (950 g) lamb fillets
1 bunch of spring onions
4 cloves of garlic
5 tbsp lard
4 tbsp vindaloo paste (ready made or see pg 77)
14 fl oz (400 ml) lamb stock
4 tbsp tomato puree

Preparation time: approx. 40 minutes
665 cal/2793 kJ

■ How to do it:

Wash the potatoes and cook un-peeled in salted water until firm. While waiting wash and dry the meat cut into cubes. Trim, wash and dry the onions and chop into small pieces. Melt lard in a pan and gently fry the garlic, spring onions and meat together. Add the vindaloo paste and some salt. After cooking for about 5 minutes add the lamb stock and simmer for 20 minutes. After about 10 minutes stir in the tomato purée and ground cardamom. Drain the potatoes, allow to cool, peel and cut into cubes. Finally add the potatoes to the lamb sauce in the last 5 minutes of cooking time, prepare in a bowl and serve with rice.

Lamb fillet

The fillet of a lamb is by far the best piece of meat. The meat is tastier if it originates from a somewhat older animal giving it a better aroma and colour.

Potatoes

"Aloo" as they are known in India, arrived together with the Europeans in the 16th century. Since then potatoes have become a regular ingredient in a large part of the cuisine.

A REAL POULTRY TREAT

Poultry Dishes

Having any kind of poultry to cook for your dinner in India very much depends on whether you can afford it or not. It is therefore a special occasion when it appears on your plate and fittingly there are great recipes to honour this. If the poultry is already skinned this is an advantage, allowing the seasoned marinade to infuse its full spicy flavour into the meat. The meat is traditionally prepared in small pieces so that everyone gets a fair share of this special treat.

CHICKEN TANDOORI

Serves 4

1 poulard
2 fl oz (50 ml) lemon juice
1 tbsp salt
2 tbsp each: coriander and
cumin seeds
10 cloves
5 red onions
5 cloves of garlic
2 tbsp freshly grated ginger
2 tbsp chilli powder
1 tbsp ground turmeric
10–11 oz (300 g) yoghurt
4 tbsp cream
4 tbsp tandoori paste
butter, for greasing tray

Preparation time: approx. 50 minutes
(excluding cooling time)
590 cal/2478 kJ

Tandoori paste

*This hot and spicy red paste is a
very characteristic ingredient of
the Indian culinary form. Particularly favoured for the enhanc-
ement of many poultry dishes.
Tandoori paste is a blend of
tamarind, coriander, cumin,
garlic, ginger and other Asian
spices. You should always have
some handy.*

■ **How to do it:**

Cut the meat into large pieces, wash
it and dry it. Mix the salt and the
lemon juice together and brush this
onto the meat. Leave to stand for
1 hour. While waiting dry roast the
coriander, cumin, and cloves in a
pan until they start to give off a
strong aroma. Allow the blend to
cool and then grind. Peel the onions
and cut into cubes. Peel the garlic
and chop up finely. Mix both with
the ginger and liquidise with a hand-
blender. Stir in the ground turmeric,
chilli powder, yoghurt, cream, your
ground spices and of course the tandoori paste. Brush the mixture onto
the pieces of chicken and place them
in a large bowl, and leave to steep
for at least 8 hours. Preheat the oven
to gas mark 3, 325 °F (170 °C).
Grease a dripping tray with butter
and spread the meat out onto it.
Place in the middle of the oven and
roast for approximately 30 minutes.
Occasionally turn the meat over.
Serve together with bread and
chutney.

1 Brush the meat with the lemon
juice mix.

2 Dry roast the spices in a pan.

3 Liquidise the onion, garlic and ginger with a hand-blender.

4 Brush the poulard pieces with the yoghurt-spice mix.

DUCK KORMA

VARIATION

Try using cooked chickpeas instead of the duck breast. Gently fry with the paste and follow the rest of the recipe as normal. Serve with tomato wedges.

Serves 4

4 tbsp sunflower oil
1 tbsp cardamom seeds
1 tbsp cumin seeds
2 tbsp poppy seeds
1 tbsp mustard seeds
2 tbsp peppercorns
4 cloves of garlic
2 tbsp freshly grated ginger
4 oz (100 g) peeled almonds
2 lb 3 oz (1 kg) duck breasts (skinned)
1 Spanish onion
4 tbsp lard
4 tbsp garam masala
3 dried chilli peppers
7 fl oz (200 ml) lamb stock
2 tbsp lemon juice
1 bunch of coriander

Preparation time: approx. 50 minutes
277 cal/1165 kJ

■ How to do it:

Roast all the seeds in a pan with the sunflower oil for about 8 minutes. Peel the garlic and chop up finely and add together with the ginger. Fry for a further 3 minutes. Leave to cool a little then liquidise together with almonds using a hand-blender. Pour on enough water to make the mixture into a smooth paste. Wash and dry the meat and cut into cubes. Peel the onions and cut also into cubes. Melt the lard in a pan and gently fry the meat with the onions on all sides. Add the almond masala and the garam masala to the meat and sprinkle with the (crushed) chilli peppers. Continue to fry for 5 minutes. Pour the lamb stock over everything, sprinkle with the lemon juice and cook on a low heat for about 15 minutes. Wash, dry and chop the coriander up finely and stir in shortly before serving.

TURKEY KEBABS

Serves 4

2 lb 3 oz (1 kg) turkey breasts
1 tbsp each: coriander, cumin,
black cumin and poppy seeds
1 tbsp each: chilli, paprika,
mustard and mango powder
1 tbsp garam masala
1 tbsp freshly grated ginger
2 tbsp chickpea flour
5 shallots
4 green chilli peppers
2 tbsp lemon juice
2 eggs
1 bunch of coriander
20 bamboo skewers
3 tbsp sunflower oil, salt

Preparation time: approx. 40 minutes
(excluding cooling time)
855 cal/3591 kJ

■ How to do it:

Wash and dry the meat, chop into
small pieces and run through a meat
grinder on a medium sized setting.
Dry roast the seeds and spices together in a pan, allow them to cool
and then grind together. Add to the
meat and mix together with the flour
and ginger. Peel the shallots and cut
into cubes. Wash the chilli peppers
and cut in half, remove seeds and
chop up finely. Add the shallots and
chilli to the meat; sprinkle with the
lemon juice and allow to cool for
about 30 minutes. Whisk the eggs in
a bowl. Wash, dry and finely chop
the coriander and sprinkle over the
eggs. Add some salt to taste. Briefly
soak the bamboo skewers in water.
Mix the eggs with the meat mass.
Form 20 small meat rolls and skewer
them. Heat up the oil and fry for
about 10 minutes, turning regularly.

Almonds

Almonds are the kernels that have been removed from the very hard stone fruit of the almond tree. They have a very fine nutty taste, and boiling them in water, allows the peel to be easily removed.

Pistachios

Pistachios, also known as green almonds, are taken from the stone fruit of the evergreen pistachio tree. The bright green, hazelnut sized kernels are ideal for decorating and are also used as seasoning for many a meat and poultry dish.

Walnuts

Walnuts were introduced to Indian cooking by Persian travellers. They are very high in protein, vitamins and minerals and, unlike in our cuisine, are also used in somewhat heavier tasting dishes.

Sultanas

Sultanas are made out of light coloured grapes and get a yellowish-green colour when they are dried. They are also sometimes referred to as golden raisins.

ROASTED CHICKEN

Serves 4

2 broilers
3 tbsp ground paprika
4 tbsp garam masala
Butter, for the dripping tray
6 shallots
3 tbsp lard
1 small bag of saffron threads
14 oz (400 g) yoghurt
4 oz (100 g) peeled almonds
4 oz (100 g) (shelled) pistachio nuts
4 oz (100 g) walnuts
4 oz (100 g) sultanas
1 tbsp ghee

Preparation time: approx. 1 hour
1657 cal/6961 kJ

■ **How to do it:**

Preheat the oven to gas mark 4, 350 °F (180 °C). Wash and dry the meat. Mix the ground paprika and garam masala together and rub into the meat. Grease the dripping tray with some butter and place the chickens on it.

Slide onto the middle shelf of the oven and roast for about 50 minutes. While the chicken is cooking, peel the shallots and cut into cubes. Melt the lard in a pan and gently fry the shallots. Add the saffron threads and yoghurt and simmer for 4 minutes. Pour the mixture over the chickens after they have roasted for 20 minutes, and continue to cook. Now lightly fry the almonds, pistachios, walnuts and sultanas in some heated ghee and liquidise it with a hand-blender. Remove the chickens, cut in half and decorate with the nut mixture and serve. Saffron rice goes well with this.

1 Rub the spice blend into the meat.

2 Gently fry the shallots in heated lard.

3 Add saffron and yoghurt.

4 Pour the mixture over the chickens.

STUFFED SAVOY CABBAGE

Serves 4

3/4 lb (800 g) savoy cabbage
salt
3/4 lb (800 g) chicken breast
fillets
6 cloves of garlic
6 tbsp sunflower oil
2 tbsp freshly grated ginger
1 tbsp ground turmeric
3 tbsp garam masala
4 tbsp lemon juice
chilli powder, pepper
14 oz (400 g) tinned peeled
tomatoes
7 oz (200 g) yoghurt
3 tbsp cream

Preparation time: approx. 35 minutes
500 cal/2100 kJ

■ How to do it:

Select 16 good leaves from the
savoy cabbage, wash and blanch
them in lightly salted water for
3 minutes. Rinse under cold water
and drain. Spread leaves out flat on
a working surface. Chop the remaining cabbage into strips. Wash, dry
and roughly chop up the chicken fillets. Mince in a meat grinder on a
medium setting. Peel the onions and
cut them into cubes. Peel the cloves
of garlic and chop up finely. Heat

the oil in a pan and gently fry the
chicken, garlic, onions and cabbage
strips together. Season the meat with
the ginger, turmeric, garam masala,
lemon juice, chilli powder and salt
and pepper. Gently fry for a further.
8 minutes. Separately heat up tinned
tomatoes with their juice and gradually stir in the yoghurt and cream.
Deal out portions of the meat mass
onto each flattened cabbage leaf
and roll up into parcels. Place the
rolls on plates with the tomato sauce
poured over and serve with rice.

KASHMIR DRUMSTICKS

Serves 4

4 cloves of garlic
6 red onions
4 tbsp olive oil
1/2 tbsp black pepper
1/2 tbsp ground cardamom
1 tsp ground cinnamon
1 tsp ground cumin
1/2 tsp ground cloves
a few saffron threads
16 chicken drumsticks
1 tbsp chilli powder
2 tbsp paprika powder
9 oz (250 g) yoghurt
3 tbsp double cream

Preparation time: approx. 30 minutes

405 cal/1701 kJ

■ How to do it:

Peel the cloves of garlic and chop up finely. Peel the onions and cut into cubes. Heat up the oil in a pan, add the garlic, onions, pepper, cardamom, cinnamon, cumin and cloves and fry gently. Add the saffron threads. Wash and dry the meat and add to the spice blend. Season everything with the chilli and paprika powder and cook on a low heat for approximately 10 minutes. Little by little stir in the yoghurt and double cream. Cook for another 5 minutes. Dress a plate with the cooked meat and serve with rice (saffron rice goes very well with this).

Paprika powder

Paprika powder is a strong red colour. The fine sweet paprika has a mild flavour, whereas rose paprika is much spicier.

Chilli powder

The powder is derived from dried chilli peppers and has a dark rich red colour. This hot and spicy season has lots of admirers in Europe. It is a very practical alternative, when no fresh chilli peppers are to be had.

SPICY LEG OF DUCK

Serves 4

4 tbsp cumin seeds
10 dried red chilli peppers
2 tbsp black pepper corns
2 tbsp cardamom seeds
1/2 tbsp black caraway seeds
1 tbsp pimento seeds
2 cinnamon sticks
(approx. 2 inches/5 cm)
2 tbsp black or yellow mustard
seeds
2 tbsp fenugreek seeds
8 legs of duck
2 lb 3 oz (1 kg) fresh spinach
leaves
salt
4 green chilli peppers
4 Spanish onions
3 cloves of garlic
5 tbsp lard
2 tbsp freshly grated ginger
1 tsp ground turmeric
4 oz (100 g) tinned peeled
tomatoes
4–5 tbsp yoghurt
dripping, for frying

Preparation time: approx. 1 hour
557 cal/2341 kJ

Spinach

*You can usually buy root or leaf
spinach fresh. Root spinach is the
name given to the crop when the
whole plant is harvested, as op-
posed to just the leaves.*

■ How to do it:

To create the right mix of seasoning,
dry roast all the spices from the
cumin seeds to the fenugreek seeds
in a pan for 3–5 minutes, stirring
continuously until they start to turn
brown. Leave to cool and then
grind. Wash, dry and skin the leg
of duck. Slice the meat open and
rub the spice mixture into it. Leave
for 20 minutes. While waiting prepare the spinach by washing it,
trimming the coarse stems off and
blanching it in boiling salted water
for 3–4 minutes. Remove from the
water, drain and chop up roughly.
Trim and wash the chilli peppers, cut
lengthways and remove the seeds.
Peel the cloves of garlic and onions.
Cut into small cubes and gently fry
in the melted lard for 3–4 minutes.
Add the ginger, ground turmeric
and the tomatoes with their juices.
Stir and simmer everything for
2–3 minutes. Fold yoghurt in
slowly. Add spinach and salt to
taste and leave to simmer for another 4–6 minutes, occasionally stirring. Keep vegetables warm. Heat
the dripping up in a pan and fry
the duck's legs on all sides for
15–20 minutes. Prepare the duck
on a bed of the spinach mixture
and serve.

1 Remove skin from duck meat.

2 Blanch the spinach in boiling water.

3 Stir the yoghurt into the tomato mixture.

4 Fry the leg of duck in hot dripping.

POULTRY TIKKA

VARIATION

You can achieve a slightly different taste by frying the meat without the skewers and then pouring 5–6 tbsp marsala over it. Allow the flavour to cook in for a while and prepare similarly, serving with rice or bread.

Serves 4

2 lb 3 oz (1 kg) chicken or turkey breasts (skinned and boned)
4 cloves of garlic
2 tbsp freshly grated ginger
2 tbsp ground coriander
1 tbsp chilli powder
1 tsp each: clove and mustard powder
4–5 tbsp each: lemon juice and chopped fresh coriander leaves
9 oz (250 g) yoghurt
2–3 tbsp cream
1–2 tsp salt
wooden skewers
dripping, for frying
lemon, onion and tomato slices, to decorate

Preparation time: approx. 20 minutes (excluding cooling time)
377 cal/1585 kJ

■ How to do it:

Wash and dry the meat, and cut into medium-sized cubes. Peel the cloves of garlic and mix all of the ingredients up to and including the salt together, stirring into a sauce. Put the meat in a bowl and slowly pour the marinade sauce over it, mix everything together well and leave to cool for 6–8 hours. Following this put the marinated meat on the skewers and grill or fry in a pan with some dripping. Cook well for at least 6–8 minutes. Garnish on a plate with the lemon, onion and tomato slices and serve.

HOT & SOUR CHICKEN WITH BEANS

Serves 4

1 lb 2 oz (500 g) mung beans
500–750 ml18 fl oz–1 pint 7 fl
oz (500–750 ml) poultry stock
1/2 tbsp ground turmeric
1 tbsp freshly grated ginger
1/2 tsp asafoetida (available in
most shops)
1 lb 11 oz (750 g) chicken
breasts (skinned and boned)
4 Spanish onions
1 piece fresh ginger
(approx. 2 inches/5 cm)
8 cloves of garlic
6–7 tbsp lard
4 tbsp hot seasoning marinade
(see recipe page 98)
4 tbsp white wine vinegar
1 tbsp ground turmeric
1 tbsp paprika powder
1 tbsp ground coriander
1 tsp salt

Preparation time: approx. 30 minutes
(excluding soaking time)
492 cal/2068 kJ

■ **How to do it:**

Select the best beans and leave to
soak in cold water for 1 1/2–2
hours. Following this drain the remaining water and allow the beans
to drip-dry. Mix the spices into the
poultry stock, add the beans and
cook for 15–20 minutes. Wash and
dry the meat and cut into thin strips.
Peel the onions, cloves of garlic and
ginger and cut into small cubes. Melt
the lard in a pan and fry the cubes
for 3–4 minutes. Stir in the unused
remaining ingredients including the
marinade and braise for 3 minutes.
Add the meat and continue to cook
for 12 minutes or until the meat is firm
and tender. Drain the mung beans
and add to the mixture.
Serve immediately on a large plate.

Fenugreek

Fenugreek, known as "Methi" in India, has a strong bitter taste. The seeds are one of the spice ingredients used for curry powder.

Oranges

Oranges come in all types and sizes, and have been recently cultivated into varieties with light coloured and blood red fruit flesh.

Pomegranate

Pomegranates are fruits of a like named tree that are as large as oranges with a hard leathery brownish-red skin. The seeds can be used fresh or dried.

Mango powder

This seasoning comes from dried, unripe mangos. It has a sour piquant taste, and can be used instead of lemon juice.

STUFFED DUCK

Serves 4

1 duck (2 1/2–4 lb/1,6–2kg)
4–6 tbsp curry powder
2 bread rolls (soaked in milk and pressed out)
2 eggs
4 oz (100 g) chopped nuts
2–3 tbsp garam masala
1/2 tbsp cayenne pepper
salt
4 tbsp raisins
1 orange
1 pomegranate
2–3 tbsp lard
9 oz (250 g) poultry liver
butter, for frying
2 cloves of garlic
4 shallots
6 tbsp grenadine
2–3 tbsp ghee or lard
2 tbsp mango powder
4 tbsp curry powder
4 1/2–9 fl oz (125–250 ml) vegetable stock
1–2 tbsp chickpea flour
9 oz (250 g) natural yoghurt
2–3 tbsp cream

Preparation time: approx. 1 1/2–2 hours

1422 cal/5974 kJ

1 Crumble the rolls together with the other ingredients.

2 Add stuffing mix to the liver and fry together.

■ How to do it:

Wash and dry the whole duck. Slice crosshatching into the skin and rub the curry in well. For the stuffing crumble the rolls into small pieces. Mix together with the eggs, nuts, garam masala, pepper, salt and raisins. Peel the orange, remove the white pith from the fruit flesh and cut into small cubes. Collect excess juice. Cut the pomegranate in half and scoop out the seeds. Add half of the seeds and the orange to the bread mass and mix everything together. Preheat the oven to gas mark 4, 350 °F (180 °C). Melt the lard in a pan and gently fry the roughly cut liver pieces for 2–4 minutes. Add the rest of the stuffing mix and fry for another 3–4 minutes while stirring. Leave to cool briefly and then fill the duck with the completed stuffing. Put in a casserole dish and fry well on all sides. Place the duck in the oven, breast facing upward on a grate over the dripping tray and roast for 60–85 minutes. Occasionally brush over with the fat dripping off or some butter. While the duck is roasting peel the cloves of garlic and the onions and liquidise. Mix together with the orange juice, grenadine and ghee and fry gently while stirring for 2–3 minutes. Stir in the mango and curry powder and simmer for a further 2 minutes. Mix the flour into the vegetable stock, add to the rest of the sauce mixture and bring to the boil. Remove from the heat and stir in the yoghurt and cream when the sauce has stopped bubbling. Sprinkle the rest of the pomegranate seeds onto the sauce and serve together with the duck.

POULTRY BIRYANI

Serves 4

2 Spanish onions
2 cloves of garlic
1 tbsp fresh grated ginger
2–3 tbsp garam masala
9 oz (250 g) natural yoghurt
1–2 tbsp cream
1–2 tbsp salt
8–10 chicken thighs
4 tbsp smooth almonds
4 tbsp chopped cashew nuts
6–7 tbsp ghee or lard
1 frying onion
10–11 oz (300 g) Patna or red Indian rice
6–7 cloves
1 tbsp ground turmeric
1 tbsp black pepper corns
6–7 green cardamom pods
1 tbsp ground cardamom
1 cinnamon stick

4–5 bay leaves
1 pint 15 fl oz (1 l) vegetable stock
1/2 saffron powder
2–3 tbsp butter
red chilli peppers and fresh coriander leaves, to garnish

Preparation time: approx. 1 hour 10 minutes
1192 cal/5008 kJ

■ **How to do it:**

Peel the cloves of garlic and onions and liquidise with the all the spice ingredients in a blender. Remove skin from chicken thighs. Wash and dry the meat and cut slices into the flesh. Rub the blended spices into the chicken and leave for 20–25 minutes to absorb the flavours. While waiting mix the nuts together. Heat up half of the ghee and roast the nuts until brown. Take out, allow them to dry, and place to one side. Peel the onions and chop up finely. Melt the rest of the ghee in a pan and gently fry the onions for 3–4 minutes. Add the chicken thighs and fry on all sides for 5–6 minutes. Put the rice in a sieve and wash with cold running water until it drains off clean. Add to the meat, sprinkle with the spices and pour over with the vegetable stock. Stir everything well together and cook at a moderate heat for 15–20 minutes until the liquid is completely absorbed. Stir in the saffron and butter and sprinkle with the nuts. Serve the biryani on plates, garnished with chilli peppers and coriander leaves.

CHICKEN MOOLEE

Serves 4

4 chicken breast fillets
5 tbsp sunflower or peanut oil
6 shallots
3 cloves of garlic
4 green chilli peppers
8 green cardamom pods
8 cloves
1 cinnamon stick
9 oz (250 g) pineapple cubes
5 tbsp pomegranate
1 tbsp ground turmeric
3 tbsp crushed peanuts
6–8 tbsp thick and sweet
coconut cream
3 tbsp freshly grated ginger
4 1/2–9 fl oz (125–250 ml)
vegetable stock
mint and alfalfa sprouts,
to garnish

Preparation time: approx. 40 minutes
462 cal/1942 kJ

■ **How to do it:**

Remove the skin from the chicken breast fillets and wash and dry the meat. Heat up the oil in a pan and fry the chicken for 3–4 minutes on both sides. Remove from the heat and place to one side. Peel the shallots and cloves of garlic and chop up finely. Clean the chilli peppers, cut in half lengthways and remove the seeds. Cut the chilli peppers into small cubes. Mix the onions, shallots and chilli with the spices into the oil and fry for about 4 minutes while stirring. Put the pineapple cubes into a sieve and drain. Chop the fruit flesh up finely. Mix together with the pomegranate, ground turmeric, peanuts, coconut cream and ginger. Stir all this into the ingredients in the pan and simmer for about 3 minutes. Add the meat, pour over the poultry stock and cook for a further 10 minutes. Stir occasionally and add vegetable stock when necessary. Serve while still very hot, garnished with the alfalfa sprouts and mint.

Peanuts

Peanuts are actually considered, in botanical terms, almost to be a root vegetable because the seed pods ripen underground. They are however categorised as a nut, due to their taste.

Pineapple

Pineapples or "Royal Tropical Fruit" are originally from America and are not a typically Indian fruit, but are well established in the cuisine. This very juicy fruit can mostly be purchased all year around and is available in all sizes, from baby pineapples to 3 kg ones.

POULTRY MAKHANI

Serves 4

2 lb 3 oz (1 kg) chicken or
turkey breasts
6 cloves of garlic
4 green chilli peppers
2 tbsp roasted cumin seeds
1 tbsp roasted black cumin
seeds
2–3 tbsp garam masala
1–2 tsp salt
4 tbsp freshly chopped coriander leaves
5 tbsp lemon juice
1–2 tbsp pineapple juice
9 oz (250 g) natural yoghurt
2 lb 10 oz (1,2 kg) leaf tomatoes
3–4 tbsp tomato juice
6–7 tbsp ghee or butter
1 tbsp brown sugar
salt
pepper
9 oz (250 g) sour cream
oil, for frying
2–3 tbsp double cream
fresh coriander leaves,
to garnish

Preparation time: approx. 1 hour
540 cal/2268 kJ

■ How to do it:

Remove the skin from the meat, wash
and dry it and chop into thin strips.
Put all the ingredients up to and including the natural yoghurt in a
blender and liquidise to a fine consistency. Put the meat into a flat
large bowl and pour the marinade
over it. Put in the fridge and let it
steep for about 25 minutes. While
waiting prepare the sauce. Start by
washing the tomatoes and cutting
them into quarters then pour over
with the tomato juice and cook for
14 minutes until the tomatoes disinte-
grate. Pour everything through a
sieve. Melt the butter and add the
tomato purée, sugar, salt and pepper and cook gently for 6–8 minutes. Finally stir in the sour cream
and put the sauce to one side. Remove the meat from its marinade
and put in a pan and fry in hot oil
for 4 minutes on all sides. Then add
the marinade and cook for a further
3–4 minutes. Take off the heat; add
the tomato sauce and mix everything well. Stir in the double cream.
Serve immediately, garnished with
the fresh coriander leaves.

Tomatoes

*It is the thick tomato sauce that
gives the makhani its typical taste.
Fleshy tomatoes on their stalks are
ideal for this recipe.*

1 Remove the skin from the poultry
breast.

2 Chop the meat into thin strips.

3 Pour the marinade over the meat.

4 Fry the meat in hot oil in a frying pan.

DUCK BREASTS WITH APRICOTS

VARIATION

Liquidise the garlic, ginger and chilli peppers and brush it onto the meat. Fry the duck breast with a seasoning of ground turmeric, cumin, salt and pepper.

Serves 4

2 lb 10 oz (1,2 kg) duck breasts
4 cloves of garlic
2 tbsp freshly grated ginger
3–4 tbsp garam masala
1 tbsp chilli powder
14 oz (400 g) dried apricots
9 oz (250 g) poultry stock
6 shallots
6–7 tbsp sunflower oil
10–11 oz (300 g) tinned peeled tomatoes
1 tsp salt
1 tbsp brown sugar
2–3 tbsp raspberry vinegar
3–4 tbsp chopped, roasted pine nuts

Preparation time: approx. 30 minutes
(excluding cooling time)
553 cal/2320 kJ

■ How to do it:

Remove the skin from the duck breasts. Wash and dry the meat and cut into strips. Peel the cloves of garlic and chop up finely. Mix together with the ginger, garam masala and chilli powder. Add the meat strips, mix everything and leave to stand in a cool place for 1 hour. Chop the apricots into cubes and put to soak in the stock for approximately 1 hour. Following this peel the shallots and chop up finely. Heat the oil and gently fry the shallots for about 3 minutes. Add the strips of duck and fry for approximately 5 minutes stirring continuously. Add the apricot stock and all the other remaining ingredients apart from the pine nuts, stir everything together and cook for a further 6 minutes. Serve immediately, sprinkled with pine nuts.

POULTRY KAFFA WITH YOGHURT

Serves 4

2 lb 10 oz–3 lb 5 oz
(1,2 kg–1,5 kg) poultry
6–7 slices of toast
3 each: red and green chilli
peppers
4 red onions
2 tbsp freshly grated ginger
2 eggs
1 tbsp each: ground coriander
and cumin
salt
pepper
fat, for deep frying
1 lb 2 oz (500 g) natural yoghurt
4–5 tbsp cream
4 tbsp chopped fresh mint
mint leaves, to garnish

Preparation time: approx. 45 minutes
355 cal/1491 kJ

■ **How to do it:**

Bone the meat and remove the skin.
Roughly cut meat into pieces (you
can use the bones, skin, and other
poultry remains to make your own
stock). Mince the meat together with
the bread, the cleaned, de-seeded
chilli peppers, the peeled onions
and the ginger, using a meat grinder
on a fine cut setting. Knead the eggs
into the mass and season with the
coriander, cumin, salt and pepper.
With wet hands, form the mass into
small balls. Put into heated oil and
deep fry for about 6 minutes until
golden brown. Use a kitchen towel
to catch the excess oil from the
balls. Stir the cream, salt and mint
into the yoghurt. Prepare the poultry
balls on a large plate, garnish with
mint leaves and serve.

A CUT OF LEG, OFF THE SKEWER OR TENDER CHOPS

Lamb Dishes

Due to the variety of religious beliefs, this meat is consumed in India in many different forms or not at all. There is a strong Muslim community in India as well as a Christian minority in west India and of course the Hindu majority that is distributed everywhere. All of these different faiths have their own preferences and taboos. Hindus are particularly against the consumption of beef, resulting in a large selection particularly of lamb and goats meat dishes all over India. The following lamb dishes can also be prepared with young goats meat. If they do not have a particular religious significance for you then beef or pork can also be used.

Leg of lamb

The leg of a young animal weighs anything from 3–5 1/2 lb (1 1/2–2 1/2 kg) and has a good red meat, with cream coloured tender strands of fat running through it. The fat is very important in absorbing the aroma and keeping the meat juicy during cooking.

Pimento corns

The corns are either dark red or blackish-brown and have a taste somewhere between cloves and pepper. Also known, therefore as clove pepper or seasoning corn. Pimentos are one of the spices that form the basis for curry powder.

Aniseed

Aniseed is known as "Soaf" in India which at the same time is the name given to fennel seeds. This is probably due to the fact that both of these plants give off the same unmistakable sweet aroma. In Europe the smell is mostly associated with spicy teas and Christmas baking.

Brown cane sugar

Brown cane sugar is derived from sugar cane grown in tropical regions. It has a stronger aroma and is much healthier than white refined sugar, that itself is derived from sugar beet. Brown sugar thickens very quickly as well.

RAAN – LEG OF LAMB

Serves 4

4–5 lb (1.8–2.2 kg) leg of lamb
3–4 oz (80 g) ground ginger
10 cloves of garlic
2 tbsp grated lemon peel
1/2 tsp pimento corns
1 tbsp aniseed
4 1/2 fl oz (125 ml) lemon juice
1 tbsp cumin seeds
1/2 tbsp cardamom seeds
1/2 tbsp ground cloves
1 tbsp ground turmeric
1 tbsp salt
9 oz (250 g) natural yoghurt
7–9 oz (200–250 g) whole, unpeeled almonds
6 tbsp brown cane sugar
1 tsp saffron powder
6–7 tbsp lamb stock
mint leaves, to garnish

Preparation time: approx. 2 hours 15 minutes (excluding marinating time)
405 cal/1701 kJ

■ **How to do it:**

Remove the skin and top fat from the leg of lamb. Wash and dry the meat and crosshatch it with a sharp knife. Peel the ginger and cloves of garlic and place into a bowl. Add all the ingredients from the lemon peel up to and including the salt. Liquidise to a fine purée using a hand-blender. Place the leg of lamb into an ovenproof dish and rub the spice paste well into the meat. Leave to marinate for 40–50 minutes in a cool place. Following this mix the yoghurt, almonds and cane sugar together and brush the resulting mixture over the lamb. Cover and leave overnight. On the next day preheat the oven to gas mark 8, 450 °F (220 °C). Place the lamb on the middle shelf and roast for 25–35 minutes. Cover with aluminium foil and cook at gas mark 1–2, 175–200 °F (150–160 °C) for a further 80–90 minutes. Stir the saffron powder into the stock and pour over meat. Cook without a cover for another 10–15 minutes. Take the lamb out of the oven, cover up and leave to stand for 5–8 minutes. Pour the juices out of the casserole through a sieve and heat up. Dress the lamb with the sauce and garnish with the mint leaves.

1 Cut crosshatching into the top of the meat.

2 Liquidise the ingredients with a hand-blender.

MURGHAL MASALA CHOPS

Serves 4

8 lamb chops
1/2 tsp ground cardamom
1/2 cinnamon stick
2 cloves of garlic
1 tsp black pepper corns
1/2 tsp freshly grated nutmeg
1/2 tsp chilli powder
3 tbsp olive oil
1 tsp lemon juice
chicory, tomatoes and 4 tbsp
alfalfa, to garnish

Preparation time: approx. 20 minutes
265 cal/1113 kJ

■ **How to do it:**

Wash and dry the meat and put to one side. Add the ground cardamom, cinnamon stick, cloves of garlic, peppercorns, nutmeg and chilli powder to a mortar and crush down to a fine paste. Brush the resulting paste onto the meat. Heat the oil in a pan and fry the chops in it for about 5 minutes. Sprinkle over the lemon juice and cook for a further 3 minutes. Wash and dry the chicory and break off individual leaves. Wash and dry the tomatoes and cut into wedges. Decorate a plate with the lamb, chicory, tomatoes and the alfalfa on top and serve. Naan bread goes well with this dish.

LAMB WITH MINT AND ALMONDS

Serves 4

2 lb 3–12 oz (1–1.3 kg)
shoulder of lamb
14 oz (400 g) natural yoghurt
6 Spanish onions
4 cloves of garlic
6–7 tbsp lard
4 green chilli peppers
1 red chilli pepper
1 piece fresh ginger
(approx. 3 inches/7 cm)
2 tbsp coriander seeds
1 tbsp cumin seeds
1 1/2 bunches of fresh mint
1/2 bunch of fresh coriander
leaves
8 green cardamom pods
8 cloves
2 cinnamon sticks
salt
2 tbsp black and white mustard
seeds
1 tbsp oil
14 oz (400 g) almond leaves
thai basil, to garnish

Preparation time: approx. 25 minutes

1233 cal/5201 kJ

■ **How to do it:**

Bone meat and trim off the skin, fat
and tendons. Wash, dry and chop
into medium sized cubes. Mix with
half of the yoghurt. Peel the onions
and cloves of garlic and chop up
finely. Melt 4 tbsp of the lard in a
pan and fry the onions in it for
3–4 minutes. Add the meat and stir
in, frying on all sides for 10–12 minutes. Wash the chilli peppers and
chop up finely. Mix together with
the garlic, the other half of the yoghurt and all the herbs and spices
up to and including the green coriander leaves and put them all into
a blender and liquidise to a fine
purée. Melt the rest of the lard in
a deep pan and gently fry the
cardamom, cloves and cinnamon
sticks for 4–5 minutes. Stir in the yoghurt paste and cook for a further
3–4 minutes. Add the meat. Add
salt according to taste and cook for
a further 12–15 minutes. Fry the
mustard seeds in the oil for about
3–4 minutes until the pods burst
open. Gently press them with a
fork and add to the meat for the
last 5 minutes. Dry roast the almonds in a pan. Serve the lamb on
a plate, sprinkled with the almonds
and garnished with the thai basil.

Black mustard seeds

The very dark brown corns of the
mustard plant have a very strong,
biting taste.

White mustard seeds

More accurately speaking these
corns are the yellow seeds of white
mustard. They are somewhat milder
than their black counterparts and
taste a bit like horseradish with a
slightly burning aftertaste.

FEAST DAY LAMB

Serves 4

5 oz (120 g) each: red lentils,
chickpeas and mung beans
2 lb 3 oz (1 kg) leg of lamb
1 1/2 pints (900 ml) lamb stock
salt
12 oz (350 g) aubergines
10–11 oz (300 g) pumpkin
7 oz (200 g) potatoes
4 plum tomatoes
4–5 tbsp lard
7 cloves of garlic
1 piece of ginger
(approx. 2–3 inches/6–7 cm)
1 bunch of fresh coriander leaves
1/2 bunch of fresh mint
3 tbsp ground cumin
2 tbsp ground cardamom
1/2 tbsp grated fenugreek seeds
2 tbsp ground turmeric
1/2 ground cinnamon
4 tbsp tomato purée
pepper
1 Spanish onion
1 tbsp mustard powder
fresh mint, to garnish

Preparation time: approx. 25 minutes
(excluding soaking time)
810 cal/3402 kJ

Split red lentils
*Split red lentils are known in India
as Masur dal, and are light red
with a mild aroma. Upon cooking
they turn yellow or light orange.
They can be obtained in most well
stocked supermarkets or health
food shops.*

■ How to do it:

Soak the pulses for 6–8 hours. Bone
the meat and trim off the skin, excess
fat and tendons. Wash and dry the
meat and cut into cubes. Drain the
pulses through a sieve and allow to
drip-dry completely. Add the pulses
and meat to a large pot and pour
over the stock until it covers everything. Add plenty of salt. Bring to
the boil and then reduce to a medium heat and cook for 18–22 minutes. Occasionally scoop off any
foam that develops on the surface.
Trim, wash and (if necessary) peel
the vegetables and chop up coarsely. Remove the meat using a spoon
or ladle and put to one side. Add the
vegetables to the pulses and continue to cook for another 10–16 minutes. Liquidise everything to a rough
purée with a hand-blender. Peel the
cloves of garlic and chop up finely.
Peel and grate the ginger. Wash and
chop up the coriander and mint finely. Liquidise the garlic, ginger and
herbs with the hand-blender. Heat
up gently for 2 minutes and then add
the rest of the seasoning up to and
including the tomato purée and gently heat for a further 2 minutes. Add
the meat and the vegetable purée
to the seasoning with adequate salt
and pepper to taste and cook for
a further 10–12 minutes. Peel the
Spanish onions and cut into thin
slices. Fry gently in some oil until
golden brown. Place to one side.
Shortly before the lamb is ready
add the mustard powder. Serve the
feast day lamb garnished with the
Spanish onions and mint.

1 Drain the pulses through a sieve.

2 Occasionally scoop off the foam from the meat stock.

3 Add the vegetables to the pulses.

4 Liquidise everything with the hand-blender.

BRAISED LAMB KEBABS

VARIATION

Try making a marinade out of the sauce ingredients (without the stock) and plus 2–3 tbsp each of garam masala and white wine vinegar. Marinate the meat and then skewer and grill it.

Serves 4

3/4 lb (800 g) lamb fillet
7 oz (200 g) pearl onions
7 oz (200 g) cherry tomatoes
4 Spanish onions
2 cloves of garlic
4–5 tbsp lard
4 red chilli peppers
3–4 tbsp curry powder
2–3 tbsp tomato purée
1 bunch of fresh coriander
1–2 tbsp lemon juice
9–18 fl oz (250–500 ml) lamb stock, salt

Preparation time: approx. 40 minutes
580 cal/2436 kJ

■ How to do it:

Wash and dry the meat and cut into medium-sized cubes. Peel the pearl onions. Wash the tomatoes. Stick onto skewers alternating between the meat, onions and tomatoes. Peel the cloves of garlic and onions and chop up finely. Melt the lard in a pan and gently fry the garlic and onions for 3–4 minutes. Wash the chilli peppers and cut in half, remove seeds and chop into small cubes. Together with the chilli add the curry powder, tomato purée, finely chopped coriander, salt and the lemon juice to the onions and fry for a further 2–3 minutes. Pour the stock onto the ingredients, stir in well and then add the meat. Braise everything on a medium heat for 15–20 minutes. Remove the skewers and serve on a plate with the remaining sauce and some rice.

SPICY MINCESTEAKS

Serves 4

9 oz (250 g) black eyed beans
17 fl oz–1 pint 7 fl oz
(500–750 ml) lamb stock
1 tbsp each: ground turmeric
and freshly grated ginger
4 red onions
5–6 tbsp garam masala
4 red chilli peppers
2 green chilli peppers
1 1/2 lb (850 g) shoulder of
lamb (boneless)
12 oz (350 g) cauliflower florets
1 red bell pepper
1 bunch of spring onions
2–3 tbsp lard
salt
dripping, for frying

Preparation time: approx. 40 minutes
(excluding soaking time)
550 cal/2310 kJ

■ **How to do it:**

Wash the beans and soak for 2 hours.
After this drain through a sieve. Place
in a pot with the lamb stock, ground
turmeric and ginger. Peel the onions,
chop coarsely and add to the pot with
2–3 tbsp of the garam masala. Wash
the chilli peppers, cut in half and remove seeds. Wash the meat. Cut into
rough cubes. Add the chilli and the
meat to the beans and cook for
20–30 minutes until all the liquid is
absorbed. Pass the entire mixture
through a meat grinder and leave
to cool. Trim, wash and chop the vegetables into small cubes. Melt the lard
and gently fry them for 2–3 minutes.
Season with the salt and remaining
garam masala. Form steaks out of the
meat mass, fill with vegetables and fry
until golden. Serve with Naan bread.

Red Patna rice

Red Patna rice has thick round grains and a tender nutty taste. It is rich in carbohydrates, vitamins, minerals and trace elements.

Macis

Macis or nutmeg blossoms are the dried blossom stigmas that wrap themselves around the nutmeg. They are stronger in taste and aroma than the nut.

Black salt

Namak as it is known in Indian cooking is an interesting and very useful seasoning. Try black salt out and you will experience a unique smoked taste.

Puff pastry

Baking food in its own juices with a kind of pastry lid on top is a cooking method that has Mongolian origins.

LAMB & RICE SOUFFLÉ

Serves 4

1 lb (450 g) red Patna rice
1 pint 7 fl oz–1 pint 15 fl oz
(750–1000 ml) lamb stock
1 tbsp each: ground cumin,
cardamom and coriander
1/2 tbsp pimento powder
2 bay leaves
8 cloves of garlic
1 piece of ginger
(approx. 2–3 inches/6–7 cm)
9 oz (250 g) pine nuts
1–2 tsp nutmeg blossoms
7 cloves
1 tbsp black pepper corns
3 tbsp poppy seeds
4–5 tbsp beef stock
2 lb 3 oz (1 kg) saddle of lamb
(boneless)
6 shallots
6–7 tbsp lard
7 green cardamom pods
1 tbsp paprika powder
9 oz (250 g) yoghurt
9 oz (250 g) tinned peeled

1 Line the casserole dish with the puff pastry.

2 Make layer after layer of meat and rice.

tomatoes
salt
1 bunch of basil
dripping, to grease dish
1–2 sheets puff pastry
2–3 tbsp dried onions
egg yolk, for brushing

Preparation time: approx. 1 hour
1385 cal/5817 kJ

■ **How to do it:**

Place the rice in a sieve and wash it until the running water clears. Bring the lamb stock to the boil and add rice, spices and the peeled garlic and cook for 15–20 minutes. While waiting blend the ingredients to be used for the seasoning paste up to and including the beef stock using a mixer. Trim skin, tendons and fat off the meat, wash and dry it and cut it into strips. Peel the shallots and chop into small cubes. Melt the lard in a pan and fry for 3–4 minutes. Stir in cardamom pods and seasoning paste. Cook for a further 2–3 minutes. Add the paprika powder. Mix in the meat, yoghurt, tomatoes, salt and chopped basil. Stir in well and leave to stew for 15–20 minutes. Drain the rice thoroughly. Grease an adequately sized casserole dish. Preheat the oven to gas mark 2, 300 °F (160 °C). Roll out enough of the defrosted puff pastry and line the casserole dish with it. Add the rice and meat, alternating layer for layer. Sprinkle the dried onions on the top layer. Close off the top with a lid of puff pastry and push down firmly on the edges. Puncture the lid with a fork several times and then brush egg yolk onto it. Place on the middle shelf of the oven and bake for 18–23 minutes.

MINCEMEAT KEBABS

Serves 4

2 lb 10 oz–3 lb 5 oz
(1.2–1.5 kg) shoulder of lamb
2 Spanish onions
5 green chilli peppers
1 red chilli peppers
5 cloves of garlic
1 piece of fresh ginger
(approx. 2–3 inches/6–7 cm)
3 tbsp garam masala
1 tbsp each: ground cardamom
and coriander
1 tbsp bruised black pepper
2 tbsp chilli powder, 2 tbsp salt
3 tbsp lemon juice

2 tbsp mango powder
1 bunch of fresh coriander
leaves
2 eggs
5–6 tbsp chickpea flour
wooden skewers
oil, for grilling

Preparation time: approx. 35 minutes
(excluding standing time)
160 cal/671 kJ

■ **How to do it:**

Bone the meat and trim off the skin,
excess fat and tendons. Wash and

dry the meat and chop up into small
pieces. Place in a meat grinder together with the peeled onions, washed
chillies, peeled garlic and the ginger
and mince up finely. Knead the spices
and chopped coriander into the
mince. Add the eggs and the chickpea flour and mix well. Leave to stand
in a cool place for about 25 minutes.
Wet your hands and make 18–20
rolls out of the meat mass and then
stick them onto the skewers. Brush the
oil onto the "kebabs" and fry or grill
them until brown, making sure that
you turn them to cook all sides. Serve
with a cabbage salad.

MULTICOLOURED FILLET FRIES

Serves 4

12 oz (350 g) potatoes
5–6 tbsp lard
1 tsp caraway seeds
1 tbsp each: ground turmeric,
cumin, coriander and chilli
powder
2 cloves of garlic
12 oz (350 g) tomatoes
1 green bell pepper
1 lb 11 oz (750 g) lamb fillets
1–2 tbsp sea salt
3 tbsp garam masala
3–4 tbsp lard, for frying
7 oz (200 g) yoghurt
2–3 tbsp double cream
3–4 tbsp freshly chopped
coriander leaves

Preparation time: approx. 40 minutes
588 cal/2468 kJ

■ How to do it:

Wash and scrub the potatoes well
and cut them into thin strips. Melt the
lard in a pan and fry the potatoes
and the caraway seeds for 5–6 minutes until brown. Add the spice powders, the cloves of garlic (finely chopped), the tomatoes (skinned and cut
into cubes) and the pepper (cut into
cubes). Stir in and fry for a further
4–5 minutes. Wash and dry the
lamb fillets and cut into thin strips.
Sprinkle with the sea salt and garam
masala and allow 5–10 minutes to
marinate. Melt the lard in a pan and
gently fry the meat on all sides. Add
to the vegetables and warm up for
1–3 minutes. Mix the yoghurt with
the double cream and the chopped
coriander leaves. Dress a plate with
the fries and pour some of the yoghurt dressing on top and serve.

Caraway seeds

Also known as "Siya-Jeera", caraway seeds are predominantly used
in north Indian cuisine. Caraway
grows mostly on the slopes of the
Himalayas. It should not be confused
with cumin, which is related but has
a very different taste.

Garam masala

Garam masala must be one of India's most famous blend of spices.
A homemade mixture can have many
different variations. Ready made
blends are however available in most
supermarkets.

BRAISED MINCE

Serves 4

2 lb 10 oz (1.2 kg) shoulder of
lamb (boneless)
9 oz (250 g) red onions
5–7 tbsp lard
5 cloves of garlic
4 green chilli peppers
2 tbsp freshly grated ginger
1 tbsp ground turmeric
1 tbsp each: roasted and
crushed coriander and
caraway seeds
12 oz (350 g) tinned peeled
tomatoes
2 tbsp crushed dill seeds
salt
pepper
10–11 oz (300 g) natural
yoghurt
1 Spanish onion
2–3 tbsp oil

Preparation time: approx. 35 minutes
237 cal/994 kJ

Dill seeds

*As in Europe the leaves of the dill
plant are used in India dried and
fresh. The seeds are also used and
have a light brown colour and
look very similar to caraway
seeds.*

■ How to do it:

Trim off the skin, tendons and excess
fat from the lamb shoulder. Wash,
dry and chop up roughly. Mince the
lamb and the peeled red onions in a
meat grinder. Melt the lard in a pan
and fry the minced meat, breaking
it into smaller pieces. Peel the cloves
of garlic. Wash and trim the chilli
peppers, cut in half, remove seeds.
Chop up both into small cubes. Add
the ginger and the spices. Braise
everything together for 10–12 minutes. Add the tomatoes with their
juices, the dill seeds and the salt
and pepper. Cook on a lower heat
for 5–8 minutes. Add the yoghurt
in spoonfuls and stir into the sauce
gradually. Peel the onions and cut
into rings. Heat some oil and fry
the onions in it until they are golden
brown. Your "Kheema" is now ready
and can be served, garnished with
onion rings.

1 Fry the meat in the melted lard.

2 Add the chillies, ginger and garlic to the meat.

3 Add the tomatoes with their juices.

4 Stir in the yoghurt.

CHOPS IN HERBY-BUTTER SAUCE

VARIATION

Instead of cooking the lamb chops with butter try using 18 fl oz (500 ml) coconut milk and 1–2 tbsp wine vinegar. Dress with some sweet coconut cream and curry powder and serve.

Serves 4

6 Spanish onions
6 cloves of garlic
3 tbsp freshly grated ginger
6–7 tbsp yoghurt
4 1/2 fl oz (125 ml) lamb stock
1 tbsp each: ground coriander and cumin
2 tbsp ground turmeric
1/2 tbsp each: cayenne pepper and mustard powder
1–2 tsp salt
12 lamb chops
1 cooking onion
3–4 tbsp lard
6 tbsp butter
2 tbsp garam masala
1 bunch each: fresh coriander and mint
1 squirt of lemon juice
cucumber slices, to garnish

Preparation time: approx. 35 minutes
(excluding marinating time)
180 cal/756 kJ

■ **How to do it:**

To start with make the marinade by peeling the garlic and onions and liquidising them in a blender. Add to this the ginger, yoghurt and the rest of the marinade ingredients and stir it all together. Wash and dry the meat and make some light crosshatching cuts. Brush with the marinade and leave to steep for 40–60 minutes. Melt the lard in a pan and gently fry the (peeled and diced) onions. Add the meat and braise for 4–5 minutes. Now add the butter and garam masala. Allow the meat to stew for a further 18–20 minutes. Add the chopped herbs and the lemon juice while stirring. Serve immediately on a plate of cucumber slices.

LAMB TANDOORI

Serves 4

1 leg of lamb
(approx. 4 lb/1.8 kg)
9–10 tbsp lemon juice
1 tbsp salt
10 cloves
2 tbsp each: cumin and
coriander seeds
5 red onions
5 cloves of garlic
2 tbsp freshly grated ginger
1 tbsp each: chilli powder and
ground turmeric
10–11 oz (300 g) yoghurt
4 tbsp cream
4 tbsp tandoori paste
butter, for greasing

Preparation time: approx. 1 1/2 hours
(excluding marinating time)
225 cal/945 kJ

■ How to do it:

Bone the meat and then wash and
dry it. Roll it together and tie up using
cooking string. Sprinkle the salt onto
the lemon juice mix together and rub
into the lamb. Leave to stand for
1 hour in a cool place. Dry roast the
spices in a pan without oil, until you
can smell their aroma. Allow the
spice blend to cool down and then
grind. Peel the onions and cut into
cubes. Peel the garlic and chop up
finely. Liquidise the garlic and onion
with the ginger using a hand-blender.
Stir in the chilli, turmeric, ground spice
mix, tandoori paste, yoghurt and
cream. Rub into the meat and place
in a large bowl. Leave it to steep for
8 hours. Preheat the oven to gas
mark 3, 325 °F (170 °C). Grease
the oven's baking tray and place the
lamb on it. Slide into the middle of
the oven and roast for 30 minutes,
occasionally turning. Remove and
serve. A side dish of cabbage salad
goes well with lamb tandoori.

Morel

Cooking or pointed morels are very fine edible mushrooms with a very full flavour. You can get them fresh only around springtime. Otherwise they are available in a dried form, which is just as aromatic.

Green tomatoes

Tomatoes have been recently culti-vated so that not only red ones are available but also green and yellow. Slightly unripe red tomatoes are just as good for this recipe.

Celery seeds

Celery seeds are one of the very im-portant flavourings in Indian cooking. The seeds come from the stalk celery plant and are very small and dark col-oured with a strong caraway like taste.

Stalk celery

Indian celery is somewhat thinner than its European counterpart and is not as strong in flavour.

STEAMED MUTTON ROLL

Serves 4

Preparation time: approx. 1 3/4 hours

4 oz (100 g) dried morels
5–9 oz (150–250 g) basmati rice
18 fl oz–1 pint 7 fl oz
(500–750 ml) lamb stock
5 cloves of garlic
5 green cardamom pods
2–3 tbsp garam masala
2–3 bay leaves
1 cinnamon stick
12 oz (350 g) green tomatoes
4 shallots
2–3 tbsp sunflower oil
1 tbsp each: mustard, celery
and coriander seeds
1 tbsp sugar, 1–2 tbsp salt
9 oz (250 g) stalk celery
5 1/2 lb (2.5 kg) saddle of
a young mutton
4–5 tbsp garam masala
3 tbsp ground turmeric
1 tbsp ground turmeric and
coriander
1/2 tbsp cayenne pepper

1 Spread the filling onto the meat.

2 Roll the meat up and tie with string.

■ How to do it:

Soak the morels in water, changing it continuously to remove any sand they might contain. Allow them to swell for about 30 minutes. While waiting wash the rice and mix it in with the stock and the seasoning and cook for at least 10 minutes. Drain thoroughly and remove the non-edible seasoning. Wash the tomatoes and liquidise in a blender. Peel the shallots and chop up finely. Heat up the oil and fry the seeds for 1–2 minutes. Add the shallots, puréed tomatoes, sugar, salt and the (diced) celery. Drain the mush-rooms thoroughly, press excess water out and chop up into small pieces. Add to the filling mix and stew for 4–5 minutes. Stir the rice in gradually and allow it to cool. Bone the mutton and then wash and dry it. Cut across the meat so that you can fold it out into a large slice for a roll. Rub half of the garam masala into the meat. Spread the filling over the flat piece of meat and then make it into a rll. Fasten with the cooking string. Rub the rest of the spices into the meat. Place the meat in a steaming basket and an appropriate pot and steam for 50–60 minutes. Remove, dress and serve. Turmeric rice goes very well with this.

HOT & SPICY LEG OF LAMB

Serves 4

8–12 legs of lamb
18 fl oz (500 ml) lamb stock
salt
pepper
1 tbsp fenugreek seeds
1 tbsp black pepper corns
1/2 tbsp pimento corns
1 tbsp mustard seeds
2 tbsp cumin seeds
3 dried red chilli peppers
1 tbsp cardamom pods
1/2 cinnamon stick
1/2 ground turmeric
2 tbsp freshly grated ginger
4 chopped shallots

2 tbsp red wine or sherry vinegar
3–4 tbsp tomato purée
4–5 tbsp lamb stock
2–4 tbsp peanut oil
tomato slices, chopped spring
onions and fresh coriander
leaves, to garnish

Preparation time: 40 minutes
(plus standing time)
535 cal/2247 kJ

■ **How to do it:**

Wash and dry the lamb. Cook the
meat in the lamb stock with the salt
and 3 pints (1.5 l) of water for 15
minutes. While waiting prepare the
seasoning mixture, by taking all the
ingredients up to and including the
turmeric and dry roasting them in
a pan until you can smell their characteristic aroma. Allow to cool and
then grind. Mix the rest of the ingredients up to and including the
peanut oil and work into a smooth
paste. Remove the lamb from the
stock, allow to dry and then coat
with the paste. Place somewhere
cool and allow it to steep for
40–60 minutes. Following this grill
the legs for 14–18 minutes. Garnish
with the tomato slices, onion rings
and the fresh coriander and serve.

LAMB BIRYANI

Serves 4

2 lb 10 oz (1.2 kg) saddle of
lamb
2 tbsp cumin seeds
10 green cardamom pods
6–7 tbsp lard
7 oz (200 g) pearl onions
6 cloves of garlic
2 tbsp freshly grated ginger
12 oz (350 g) natural yoghurt
3 tbsp raisins
9 fl oz–18 fl oz (250–500 ml)
lamb stock
14 oz (400 g) basmati rice
3–4 tbsp oil
salt
pepper
1/2 tsp saffron powder
2 tbsp beetroot juice
1 bunch of basil (finely
chopped)

Preparation time: 50 minutes
743 cal/3119 kJ

■ How to do it:

Bone the meat and remove the skin
and tendons and then wash and dry
it. Cut into cubes. Melt the lard in a
pan and gently fry the cumin seeds
and cardamom pods, stirring continuously for approximately 3 minutes.
Peel the spring onions, chop up the
garlic finely and add to the spices together with the meat cubes and ginger. Mix together and fry for another
4–6 minutes. Add the yoghurt with
a spoon, stirring in gently. Add the
raisins and half of the stock. Cook
everything on a low heat for about
12 minutes. Clean and drain the rice
thoroughly. Heat the oil and sauté the
rice stirring continuously for about
5 minutes until it is glassy. Add salt
and pepper to taste and then the
meat. Pour over with the rest of the
stock and cook for approximately
15 minutes. Dish out the biryani onto
three different dishes and then colour
one with the saffron and one with
the beetroot juice and garnish the
third with the basil. Serve on a
plate or tray.

Raisins

"Raisin" is the collective term for
dried wine grapes. They are rich in
fruit sugar and vitamins. Currants
however are small, black seedless
raisins that are untreated and therefore more recommendable.

Basil

"Tulsi" as it is known in India is considered to be a sacred plant in the
Hindu culture. This wholesome herb
has a sweet peppery kind of taste.
We mostly associate it with Mediterranean cooking, but its origins lie in
fact in India and the discoverers of
yesteryear brought it to Europe.

NATURE'S GIFT

Fish and Seafood Dishes

The fine tasting fish – machi – and a never-ending assortment of seafood are considered by the people of India to be a special gift from mother nature. They come from India's abundant rivers and lakes and of course the salt waters that lap against more than 4000 km of coastline. A journey through India's machi cuisine will fill you with stimulating ideas and lots of inspiration to cook with a wide variety of exotic ingredients. Just pop down your local delicatessen or Asian shop and try out new combinations, the possibilities are endless.

CRAB

Serves 4

4 large crabs
1 pint 5 fl oz (1 l) Asian stock
1 Spanish onion
3 cloves of garlic
1 piece fresh ginger
(approx. 1 inch/2 cm)
1 beef tomato
2 green chilli peppers
3 tbsp sunflower oil
2 tbsp olive oil
2 tbsp grated coconut
1/2 tsp each: ground cumin,
cardamom and ginger powder
1/2 tsp poppy seeds
2 tbsp chopped almonds
4 fl oz (100 ml) luke warm water

Preparation time: approx. 40 minutes
318 cal/1334 kJ

The common crab

Different types and sizes of common crabs can be found in all waters around the world. They have a large flat body with a hard protective shell. The rich, tasty meat is mostly to be found in the legs of the crab.

■ **How to do it:**

Wash the crabs and then cook them in the Asian stock for about 15 minutes. While waiting peel the onions and cut into cubes. Peel the garlic and chop up finely. Peel the ginger and grate. Wash the tomato and cut into wedges. Wash the chilli peppers and cut in half, remove seeds and chop into small rings. Take the crab out of the stock, place in a sieve and drain. Carefully prise open the body shell and remove the pieces of meat. Break off the pincers and twist off the legs and likewise remove the meat. Cut into pieces. Heat the oil in a pan and gently fry the onions and garlic introducing the chillies, ginger and tomatoes and finally the crabmeat. In a bowl stir the olive oil together with the grated coconut, poppy seeds, ground turmeric, cardamom and ginger powder. Add the almonds and water and liquidise everything with a hand-blender. Pour over the crab mixture and let it draw for about 3 minutes. You can dress the ready meal in the crab shell or in bowls and serve with flat bread.

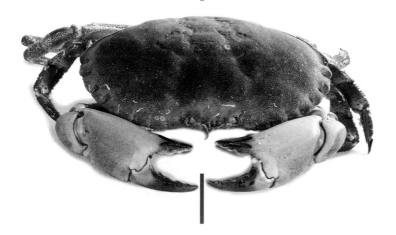

1 Carefully prise open the protective shell.

2 Remove the meat.

3 Break open the pincers.

4 Pull the meat out of the pincers.

BAKED FISH BALLS

VARIATION

Prepare the fish balls as described. You can add tomato purée to the sauce and instead of seasoning with curry leaves try chilli powder.

Serves 4

2 lb 3 oz (1 kg) fish fillet
4 tbsp lemon juice
1–2 tbsp salt
1 tbsp coarsely ground pepper
1 bunch of spring onions
1–2 eggs
4–6 oz (100–150 g) chickpea flour
4 green chilli peppers
3–4 tbsp garam masala
1 Spanish onion
4 cloves of garlic
3–4 tbsp lard
4 tbsp curry powder
2 tbsp ground turmeric
1 tbsp ground cardamom
1 tbsp each: ground turmeric and coriander
8 dried curry leaves
2 tbsp lemon juice
5 tbsp coconut flakes
1 tbsp crushed fenugreek seeds
18 fl oz (500 ml) fish stock
4 tbsp yoghurt
dripping, for greasing
basil, to garnish

Preparation time: approx. 45 minutes
570 cal/2394 kJ

■ How to do it:

Wash and dry the fish fillet and chop up finely. Mix together with the lemon juice, salt, pepper, spring onions (finely chopped) and finally the eggs. Knead in the chickpea flour. Wash the chilli peppers and cut in half, remove seeds and chop up finely. Add the chillies and the garam masala to the fish mixture. Knead the mass well and leave to stand in a cool place. Peel the cloves of garlic and onion and chop up finely. Melt the lard in a pan and gently fry them for 3–4 minutes. Preheat the oven to gas mark 4, 350 °F (180 °C). Add the spices to the pan together with the crushed curry leaves, lemon juice, coconut flakes and fenugreek seeds. Fry everything stirring continuously for 3–4 minutes. Pour the fish stock over the mixture and allow to cook a little. Slowly stir in the yoghurt spoon for spoon and keep simmering but do not boil. Grease a flat casserole dish. Make small balls out of the fish mass and place them into the casserole dish. Pour the sauce over them, place in the oven and bake for 12–16 minutes. Serve garnished with basil.

SPICY COCONUT CLAMS

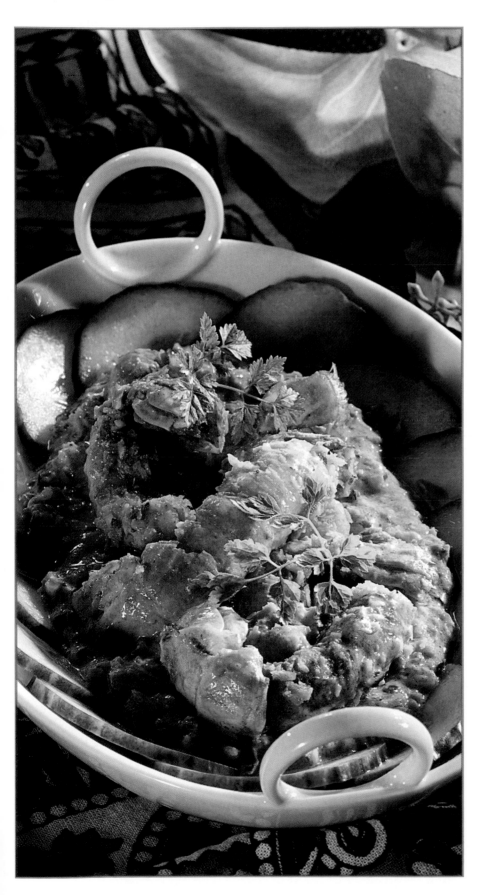

Serves 4

50–60 clams (sand mussels)
6–8 red onions
5 cloves of garlic
6–7 tbsp sunflower oil
5 tbsp coconut flakes
1 tbsp salt
2 tbsp ground turmeric
1 tbsp chilli powder
1/2 tbsp freshly ground black
pepper corns
9 fl oz (250 ml) sherry or raspberry vinegar
seaweed or crushed nori
leaves, to dress
14oz (400 g) yoghurt
4 tbsp garam masala
8 tbsp lemon juice
chervil and cucumber, to garnish

Preparation time: approx. 35 minutes

338 cal/1418 kJ

■ How to do it:

Wash the clams, trim off their beards,
and soak for 15 minutes. Dispose of
any open clams. Peel the onions and
garlic and chop finely. Heat oil in a
pan and fry the onions and garlic for
4–5 minutes. Add the coconut and
salt while stirring and fry until the ingredients start to turn brown. Add the
turmeric, chillies and pepper. Drain
the clams and add to the pan together with the vinegar. Cook everything
in a closed pot 6–9 minutes. Remove
the clams, drain and pick out pieces
of meat. Dispose of any closed clams.
Clean 24 clam shells and place on a
bed of seaweed or nori leaves. Pour
the stock through a sieve. Mix the yoghurt with the garam masala and add
to the stock. Fill the clam shells with
the meat and pour over the sauce.
Sprinkle with lemon juice and serve
with chervil and slices of cucumber.

Mussels

These mussels are amongst the most known of their kind. They have long blue-grey coloured shells and a very tasty yellow meat. They are mostly found firmly stuck to the sides of cliffs or rocks.

Squid

Squid, also referred to as calamari are a small, 5–8 cm long cuttlefish. They are usually eaten whole, but when larger, it is best to chop the cooked tentacles into rings.

Hard clam

Hard clams are small light brown pattern marked mussels with a cream coloured meat. They are mostly known from Italian cooking where they are referred to as vongole.

Shrimps

There are at least 3000 types and subtypes of shrimp spread across the oceans of the world. The names given to them are just as abundant and include; granate, crevettes, scampi, prawns, etc.

SEAFOOD BIRIYANI

Serves 4

14oz (400 g) Patna rice
1 lb 9 oz (700 g) mixed frozen seafood
18 fl oz–1 pint 7 fl oz (500–750 ml) lobster stock
400 tbsp ground turmeric
2 tbsp lemon juice
5 Spanish onions
5 cloves of garlic
5–6 tbsp of butter
3 tbsp freshly grated ginger
4 tbsp of garam masala
2 tbsp of chilli powder
4 tbsp of coconut milk
18 fl oz–1 pint 7 fl oz (500–750 ml) vegetable stock
3–4 tbsp of tomato purée

Preparation time: approx. 50 minutes
685 cal/2877 kJ

■ How to do it:

Wash and thoroughly drain the rice. Allow some time for the seafood to defrost. Following this add to it the lobster stock half of the turmeric and lemon juice and cook on a low heat for about 10 minutes. Peel the onions and garlic and chop up finely. Melt half of the butter in a pan and gently fry the onions and garlic. Stir in the ginger, garam masala, chilli powder and the rest of the turmeric and braise everything. Add the rice, coconut milk, vegetable stock and tomato purée. Stir well and leave to cook in an open pot for about 20 minutes. Melt the rest of the butter and stir fry the seafood in it for 3–5 minutes. Fold the rice in with the seafood and heat for 2–3 minutes. The biryani can now be served in a large bowl.

1 Gently fry the onions and garlic.

2 Stir in the spices.

3 Add the rice.

4 Pour the stock and coconut milk over everything.

PERCH TANDOORI

Serves 4

300 g natural yoghurt
2 tbsp chilli powder
1/2 tbsp salt
3 tbsp paprika powder
2 tbsp ground cumin
1 tbsp ground fennel seeds
4 tbsp sunflower oil
4 slices of Victoria perch
dripping, for greasing
3 Spanish onions
1 fennel bulb
1 tbsp of butter
lemon slices and fresh mint,
to garnish

Preparation time: approx. 40 minutes
(excluding marinating time)
353 cal/1481 kJ

■ How to do it:

You can make the marinade simply by stirring all of the ingredients up to and including the sunflower oil together in a bowl. Wash and dry the filets of fish and rub the marinade into them. Allow them to steep for about 6 hours. Preheat the oven to gas mark 4, 350 °F (180 °C). Grease the bottom of a casserole dish. Take the fish fillets out of the marinade and place them in the dish. Place the casserole dish on the middle shelf of the oven

and bake for 20–25 minutes. Peel the onions and slice into rings. Trim and wash the fennel, placing the leaves to one side, and then cut the bulb into thin slices. Fry the onion rings and fennel slices until slightly brown. Dress the fish with the vegetables and the lemon slices, garnish with the fennel leaves and the fresh mint and serve. Turmeric rice goes well with this.

MARINATED KING PRAWNS

Serves 4

2 lb 3 oz (1 kg) king prawns
(peeled and prepared)
4 1/2 fl oz (125 ml) lemon juice
1 tbsp salt
2 tbsp crushed green peppercorns
1 tbsp crushed aniseed
6 bay leaves
24 green cardamom pods
2 tbsp onion seeds
2 tbsp coriander seeds
2 tbsp mustard seeds
2 tbsp fenugreek seeds
5 red onions
4 cloves of garlic
2 tbsp freshly grated ginger
2 tbsp ground turmeric
14oz (400 g) yoghurt
4 1/2–9 fl oz (125–250 ml)
olive oil
2 tbsp beetroot juice
oil, for frying
lime slices and thai basil to
garnish

Preparation time: approx. 55 minutes
(excluding cooling time)
783 cal/3287 kJ

■ How to do it:

Wash and dry the prawns and place in a shallow bowl. Sprinkle with the lemon juice, salt, pepper-corns and aniseed. Leave to stand for 30 minutes. For the marinade put the spices and the seeds on a baking tray and roast in an oven set to gas mark 6, 400 °F (200 °C) for approximately 15 minutes. Allow to cool, then grind. Peel the onions and cloves of garlic and chop up roughly. Add to a mixer together with the ginger, the ground turmeric, and the yoghurt and mix well. Add the spices, oil and beetroot juice and mix well. Brush the king prawns with the marinade and leave in a cool place for 7–8 hours. Following this put the prawns on skewers and fry in oil on both sides for 4–6 minutes. Remove, dress and serve garnished with the lime slices and thai basil. Any rice goes well with this.

King prawns

King prawns, also known as tiger prawns, due to their stripy backs are found in the Pacific and Indian oceans and are a favourite in Asian cooking.

Green pepper corns

The pepper plant is a tropical climbing shrub and bears yellow, green or red berries, depending on the time of harvest. Green pepper is derived from the unripe berries that are not dried, but pickled in vinegar or salt brine directly after picking.

DEEP-FRIED SCALLOPS

Serves 4

2 lb 7 oz (2 kg) scallops
4 1/2 fl oz (125 ml) lemon juice
3–4 tbsp garam masala
2 tbsp freshly grated ginger
1 tbsp black pepper corns
10–11 oz (300 g) chickpea flour
1 pinch of baking powder
18 fl oz (500 ml) water
1 tsp ground turmeric
1/2 tbsp chilli powder
1/2 tbsp salt
3 tbsp sesame seeds
4 Spanish onions
4 green chilli peppers
2 tbsp ground coriander
1/2 tbsp ground cardamom
4–5 tbsp sunflower oil
oil, for deep-frying
lemon slices, for dressing

Preparation time: approx. 35 minutes
580 cal/2436 kJ

Scallops

Scallops are usually bought ready shelled. The white tough meat has a tender sweet taste. Gourmets particularly value the orange co-loured roe sac (corail).

■ **How to do it:**

If fresh and whole first wash and dry the scallops, prise open the shells and scoop out the meat. Place the shells to one side. Mix the lemon juice and spices together and sprinkle this on top of the scallops. Add the chickpea flour and baking powder to a mixing bowl. Stir the turmeric into the water and pour this over the flour. Work mixture into a smooth dough, and add the chilli powder, salt and sesame seeds to this. Leave to stand for a short while. Peel the onions and chop up into small cubes. Wash the chilli peppers and cut in half, remove seeds and chop up also into small cubes. Fry these together with the cardamom and coriander in the sunflower oil for 3–4 minutes. Heat the oil for deep-frying. Run the scallops through the dough, coating them thoroughly, and place them in the oil for 4–5 minutes until they are golden brown. Place a lemon slice on each mussel shell and the deep-fried scallops on top. Dress with the onion-chilli mixture and serve with some chapati bread.

1 Mix the first ingredients into a smooth dough.

2 Gently fry the chillies and onions in the sunflower oil.

3 Pull the scallops through the dough to coat them.

4 Deep-fry in hot oil until golden brown.

FISH KEBABS

VARIATION

Instead of using fish try making this recipe with peeled shrimps, king prawns or something similar. Additionally add curry powder and tomato purée to the mass. Prepare the kebabs in the same way and serve with mango chutney.

Serves 4

1 1/2 lb–2 lb 3 oz (800–1000 g) fish fillets
5 Spanish onions
4 cloves of garlic
1 piece of ginger (approx. 2–3 inches/6–8 cm)
1–2 eggs
2–3 tbsp breadcrumbs
1 tbsp each: ground cloves, coriander, cumin and aniseed
1/2 tbsp salt, pepper
1/2 tbsp freshly ground black
1–3 tbsp chickpea flour
wooden skewers
dripping, for frying
14 oz (400 g) natural yoghurt
4 tbsp cream
1 bunch of fresh mint

Preparation time: approx. 30 minutes
490 cal/2058 kJ

■ How to do it:

Wash, dry and chop the fish fillet up roughly. Peel the onions, garlic and ginger. Run everything through a meat grinder. Add the eggs, breadcrumbs and the spices and mix together into a smooth dough. Knead in the chickpea flour. Break off chunks of the dough and roll into shape. Put the rolls onto skewers. Melt the dripping in a large pan and, making sure it is not too hot, fry the kebabs, turning them on all sides for 6–8 minutes. Mix the yoghurt and cream together, finely chop the mint and add this too. Dress the fish kebabs with the yoghurt sauce and serve garnished with some mint leaves.

HOT & SPICY BAKED SARDINES

Serves 4

2 lb 3 oz (1 kg) sardines
(trimmed and ready to cook)
2–3 tbsp vinadaloo paste
(see recipe page 77)
6–7 tbsp lemon juice
6 shalotts
4 cloves of garlic
5–6 tbsp coconut flakes
4 green chilli peppers
3–4 tbsp lard
3–4 tbsp coconut milk
(unsweetened)
1 bunch of fresh coriander
2 tbsp chilli powder
4 tbsp lemon juice
7 oz (200 g) natural yoghurt
dripping, to grease ovenproof
dish
lime wedges and mint strips,
to garnish

Preparation time: approx. 45 minutes
663 cal/2783 kJ

■ **How to do it:**

Wash and dry the fish. Mix the vindaloo paste together with the lemon juice and brush onto the fish. Peel the shallots and cloves of garlic and chop into small cubes. Wash the chilli peppers and cut in half, remove seeds and chop up finely. Melt the lard in a pan and gently fry the chillies together with the coconut flakes. Add the coconut milk, fresh coriander, chilli powder and lemon juice and continue to fry gently for 6–8 minutes. Stir the yoghurt in and then remove from the heat. Preheat the oven to gas mark 2, 300 °F (160 °C). Grease a flat ovenproof dish and place the fish in it. Pour the onion-yoghurt sauce over the fish and place in the oven on the middle shelf, baking for 20 minutes. Take out of the oven, dress and serve garnished with the lime wedges and mint strips.

Mullet

Mullet live in tropical waters. Its firm white meat is very highly regarded in Asian cookery. Mullet have a high fat content and can therefore be prepared and cooked whole.

Salmon trout

Salmon trout is a good alternative to mullet because it is farmed and therefore available practically throughout the year, and also as a frozen product. The salmon trout are usually reared in salt-water pools. When fed they are usually given a carotene based supplement giving the meat a salmon-like colouring.

Sea perch

The sea perch also comes under the names of Wolf perch or Loup de mer. The white meat is very aromatic and has a low fat content. Sea perch mostly frequent coastal areas and can be fished the whole year around.

Ajowan seeds

Ajowan is an umbel plant and is related to dill, caraway and cumin. The green oval seeds look like small caraway seeds and have a pronounced sharp bitter taste.

STUFFED MULLET

Serves 4

1 mullet (trimmed and ready to cook)
6–8 tbsp lemon juice
1 tbsp ground black pepper corns
1–2 tbsp sea salt
For the stuffing:
1 lb 2 oz (500 g) potatoes
1 Spanish onion
2 tbsp freshly grated ginger
1 bunch coriander
4–5 tbsp lard
9 oz (250 g) green peas
1 tbsp ground coriander
4–5 tbsp vegetable stock
2 tbsp garam masala
1 tbsp ground cumin
1/2 tbsp cayenne pepper
3–4 tbsp lemon juice
wooden skewers, to hold together
For the seasoning paste:
1 bunch spring onions
3 cloves of garlic

1/2 tbsp ajowan seeds
1 bunch fresh coriander
7 oz (200 g) natural yoghurt
2 tbsp garam masala
1/2 tbsp each: chilli powder, ground coriander, cumin and fenugreek

Preparation time: approx. 1 1/2 hours

610 cal/2562 kJ

■ How to do it:

Wash and dry the mullet and slice open five times on both sides. Sprinkle over the lemon juice and add the salt and pepper both inside and outside. For the stuffing boil the potatoes unpeeled for about 20 minutes. While waiting peel the onions and wash the coriander and chop. Melt the lard in a pan and fry the onions with the ginger and coriander for about 4 minutes. Add the rest of the stuffing ingredients and fry for 5–6 minutes. Drain the potatoes, peel them and cut them into cubes and add to the stuffing mix, warming for about another 3 minutes. Stuff the fish with the mixture. Stick the fish together using the wooden skewers. To make the seasoning paste trim, wash and chop up the spring onions roughly. Peel the cloves of garlic. Together with the rest of the ingredients put onions and garlic in a blender and liquidise. Brush the fish on both sides with the ready masala. Place on a large piece of aluminium foil, pulling up the sides and the folding the ends together to cover the fish. Preheat the oven to gas mark 2, 300 °F (160 °C). Place the fish in the oven and bake for approximately 20 minutes. Open the foil up and turn on the grill. Grill on both sides until the mullet starts to turn slightly brown. When ready dress in portions on flat plates and serve.

1 Slice the fish open 5 times on both sides.

2 Sprinkle with salt and pepper to taste.

BRAISED PRAWNS

Serves 4

2 lb 3 oz–3 lb 6 oz
(1–1 1/2 kg) peeled prawns or
shrimps
6–7 tbsp lemon juice
3 tbsp (chopped, dry roasted)
garlic
7 oz (200 g) each: potatoes,
carrots, peas and Spanish
onions
5–6 tbsp lard
4–5 tbsp curry powder
2 tbsp garam masala
2 dried red chilli peppers
1 bunch fresh coriander
4 1/2–9 fl oz (125–250 ml)
vegetable stock
salt, pepper

Preparation time: approx. 40 minutes
258 cal/1083 kJ

■ **How to do it:**

Wash and dry the prawns and place
them in a bowl. Mix the lemon juice
with the garlic and sprinkle over the
prawns. Leave the fish to steep for
approximately 15 minutes. Trim and
wash the vegetables. Peel the potatoes, onions and carrots. Chop
everything into small cubes. Melt the
lard in a pan and gently fry the vegetables for 4–5 minutes. Add the
curry powder, garam masala, crum-
bled chilli peppers and finely
chopped coriander. Allow every-

thing to cook for 3–4 minutes. Pour
the stock in and add the prawns and
season with salt and pepper to taste.
Braise while stirring continuously for
a further 3–5 minutes. Dress on a
plate and serve.

AMOTIK — SWEET & SOUR FISH STEAKS

Serves 4

4 oz (100 g) tamarind
4 tuna fish steaks
(approx. 7 oz/200 g each)
3–4 tbsp flour
6–7 tbsp sunflower oil
2–3 mangos
1 Spanish onion
2–3 cloves of garlic
2–3 tbsp garam masala
2 tbsp mango powder
1/2 tbsp chilli powder
salt
pepper
1–2 tbsp raspberry vinegar
5–8 tbsp mango juice
thai basil, to garnish

Preparation time: approx. 25 minutes
325 cal/1368 kJ

■ How to do it:

Place the tamarind in to 4 1/2 fl oz (125 ml) of hot water and leave to soak for approximately 20 minutes. While waiting wash and dry the fish steaks, then dust them with the flour. Fry in a pan of hot oil for about 2 minutes on each side. Remove and place to one side. Peel the mangoes and chop into cubes. Peel the onions and cloves of garlic and chop up finely. Fry in the remaining fish fat for 2–3 minutes. Crush the tamarind and collect the resulting seasoned water through a sieve. Pour the tamarind water together with the garam masala, mango and chilli powder into the pan and cook everything while stirring for 4–5 minutes. Place the steaks in the sauce, sprinkle with the salt, pepper, vinegar and mango juice and simmer for 6–8 minutes. Serve on a plate together with chapatti.

Tuna fish

Tuna fish is not only good as an oil product but the fresh red meat is very tasty and rich in vitamins and minerals as well. You can obtain it all year-round mostly fresh and if not then certainly frozen.

Mango

This sweet aromatic fruit grows all over the Indian sub-continent even in uncultivated regions. Mango powder is made from the unripe, green fruit of the mango tree and is used very often in Indian cuisine.

ENCHANTING REFRESHMENT

Desserts, Pastries, Drinks and Lassis

All good things come in little packages, and these are the excellent Indian sweets that are perfect for rounding off a meal. Halva, Kulfi, Kheer and Samosas are just some of the sweet delicacies, crunchy snacks and homemade ice creams. The drinks include the omnipresent teas of India, that are served hot or chilled depending on the time of the year. Then there is of course the famous Lassi, a sour milk drink that is either sweet, with fresh herbs and salt or piquant and spicy.

CARROT HALVA

Serves 4

3/4 lb (800 g) sweet baby
carrots
1 pint 7 fl oz–1 pint 15 fl oz
(750–1000 ml) whole milk
10–12 green cardamom pods
6–8 tbsp lard
4 tbsp ground almonds
4 tbsp semolina
4 tbsp currants
2–3 tbsp maple syrup
1/2 tsp freshly grated nutmeg
10–11 oz (300 g) yoghurt
4–5 tbsp double cream
3–4 tbsp chopped almonds
1–2 tbsp rose water
yoghurt, to garnish

Preparation time: approx. 40 minutes
448 cal/1880 kJ

Carrots

*This recipe will taste the best if
you use tender, slightly sweet baby carrots or tender young carrots
still with their leaves.*

How to do it:

Peel the carrots and grate them finely. Mix with the milk and cardamom
pods and bring to the boil. Lower
heat and simmer for 18–20 minutes
stirring continuously. Remove the cardamom pods. Melt the lard in a pan
and gently roast the ground almonds
and semolina. Stir in the currants,
carrot mix and maple syrup and
continue to stir while cooking for
4–6 minutes. Add nutmeg to taste.
Mix in the yoghurt with the double
cream, chopped almonds and rose
water. Serve the Halva warm with
a dollop of yoghurt on top.

1 Roast the almonds and the
semolina.

2 Stir in the currants and carrot mixture.

3 Add nutmeg to taste.

4 Mix the yoghurt with the double cream and chopped almonds.

KULFI – HOMEMADE ICE CREAM

VARIATION

Instead of using mangos try making this with honey melons. You can even garnish the ice cream with coconut flakes and chopped fresh mint and serve it in a scooped out melon half.

Serves 4

2 lb 3 oz (1 kg) ripe mangos
3 tbsp lemon juice
5–6 tbsp maple syrup
2 tbsp each: ground cardamom, cloves and aniseed
2 tbsp freshly grated ginger
1 pint 7 fl oz (750 ml) cream
5–6 oz (150 g) finely chopped, unsalted pistachios
5–6 egg whites
star fruit slices and Melissa leaves, to garnish

Preparation time: approx. 15 minutes
(excluding cooling time)
940 cal/3948 kJ

■ How to do it:

Peel the mangos, cut in half and remove the stones. Cut the fruit flesh into cubes. Dribble the lemon juice on to the fruit and mix in the syrup and the spices and ginger and gradually warm everything up on a low heat. Stir until the syrup has dissolved. Allow time to cool, and then stir in the pistachios and cream. Put the mixture in to a bowl and leave in a freezer for 4–5 hours. Stir the half frozen mixture with a fork. Whisk the egg white into snow and fold into the ice cream mix. Dish out portions into small bowls and freeze for another 4–5 hours. Allow the ice cream to defrost a little and then decorate with the star fruit and Melissa leaves and serve.

LASSI – FRUITY SOUR MILK

Serves 4

**14 oz (400 g) frozen mixed
exotic fruits
1/2 tbsp saffron powder
1/2 tbsp each: ground
cardamom and cloves
2–3 tbsp brown sugar
1 lb 11 oz (750 g) natural
yoghurt
18 fl oz–1 pint 7 fl oz
(500–750 ml) butter milk
honey melon slices, to garnish**

Preparation time: approx. 10 minutes
328 cal/1418 kJ

■ **How to do it:**

Allow the mixed fruits to defrost slightly and then mix together with all the
other ingredients in a blender and liquidise. Fill some long glasses up to
halfway with crushed ice and fill up
the rest with Lassi. Garnish with a
slice of melon and serve immediately.

Apricots

Khubani as it is known is considered to be the golden fruit with a silk skin. Apricots represent wealth and decadence, which stems from their rareness and high price. Muslims and Persians love them in sweet dishes but also are known to cook them with meat and poultry.

Palm sugar

Palm sugar is actually a bi-product of the production of sugar from sugar cane. It is in fact the thickened, unclean juice of the crushed canes. It is very sweet and tastes similar to caramel with a light suggestion of alcohol.

Melon seeds

Melon seeds can be bought ready roasted or you can do it yourself. Simply clean them and as with pumpkin seeds lay them out on a baking tray and dry them slowly in an oven set to 120 °F (50 °C).

Rose water

Rosewater is very good for lending cream based dishes a fruity aroma. You can purchase it at the chemist or from a health food shop.

SWEET SAMOSAS

Serves 4

5–6 oz (150 g) each: wheat and rice flour
1/2 tbsp each: ground cardamom and cloves
1 tsp baking powder
4 tbsp ghee or olive oil
3 tbsp yoghurt
1–2 tsp sugar
1 lb 2 oz (500 g) fresh apricots
2 tbsp palm or brown cane sugar
1 cinnamon stick
2–4 tbsp apricot juice
1 tbsp ground cardamom
1/2 tbsp aniseed
2 tbsp melon seeds
1 lb 2 oz (500 g) cottage cheese
2–3 tbsp thick, sweet coconut cream
3–4 tbsp almond leaves
2–3 tbsp rose water
some corn flour
dripping, for baking
castor sugar, to dust

Preparation time: approx. 50 minutes
520 cal/2184 kJ

■ How to do it:

Mix together the entire dough ingredients up to and including the sugar and knead in to a smooth dough. Leave to stand for 25 minutes. To make the filling start by boiling the apricots and then peeling them, cut them in half and remove the stones and finally chop them into small pieces. Stir in to a pot with the sugar, cinnamon stick and juice and heat up while stirring for 4–5 minutes. Remove the cinnamon stick. Add the rest of the ingredients up to and including the rose water and mix together well. Roll the dough out and cut into 20 x 12 cm circles. Deal out a spoonful or so of the filling on to each one. Brush the edges with a cornflour paste and fold them together pressing the edges firmly to each other. Heat up some dripping and shallow fry them until golden brown. Dust with the castor sugar and serve.

1 Knead the ingredients into a smooth dough.

2 Chop up the peeled and seeded apricots into small pieces.

3 Add the apricots and other ingredients into a pot.

4 Deal out the filling on to each circle of dough.

KHEER – RICE PUDDING WITH BANANAS

Serves 4

5 oz (120 g) natural Patna rice
1–1 pint 15 fl oz (1–1 1/2 l)
whole milk
5 ripe bananas
4 tbsp brown sugar
3–4 tbsp double cream
1/2 oz (10 g) green cardamom
pods
2 tbsp grated lemon peel
1/2 bunch fresh mint
4 oz (100 g) sweet coconut cream
fresh mint leaves, to garnish

Preparation time: approx. 1 hour
335 cal/1407 kJ

■ **How to do it:**

Wash the rice and heat up in half
of the milk. Bring to the boil, then
reduce the heat and simmer for
35–45 minutes, until the milk has
been absorbed. While waiting peel
the bananas and mix together with
the sugar, double cream and cardamom pods and liquidise. Fold in
the grated lemon peel and finely
chopped mint. Add the banana
cream and the rest of the milk to the
rice. Stir and allow it to cool. Finally
stir in the coconut cream. Serve into
small bowls with the mint leaves.

SPICED TEA

Serves 4

1–2 tbsp cardamom pods
2 tbsp cloves
1 tbsp star aniseed
1 cinnamon stick
1 stick of liquorice
(approx. 2 inches/5 cm)
2–3 tbsp ginger powder
8–9 tbsp Assam tea
1–2 tbsp grated orange peel
milk, cream and brown cane
sugar

Preparation time: approx. 15 minutes
22 cal/923 kJ

■ How to do it:

Dry roast the cardamom, cloves, star aniseed and cinnamon in a pan without oil. Add the liquorice and approximately 1 pint 15 fl oz (1 l) water, mix together and heat up for 4–6 minutes. Add the tea, ginger powder and grated orange peel. Bring to the boil and cook for 4–6 minutes. Sieve out the tea. Add milk, cream and brown sugar to taste and serve in glass.

Liquorice

Very similar in taste to liquorice root with a bitter sweet edge and strong aroma. In Indian Ayurvedic medicine this insignificant looking plant is sworn by with the claim that it has amazing healing properties.

Assam tea

The history of tea, a stimulating infusion drink goes back a thousand years and began in the Indian province of Assam. It was taken to China where the Buddhist monks carried it further to Japan. Arabic traders brought the aromatic leaf further to Europe at the beginning of the 16th century.

CRUNCHY RINGS

Serves 4

9 oz (250 g) rice and corn flour
1–2 packets dried yeast
6–8 tbsp yoghurt
10–11 oz (300 g) brown cane
sugar
1/2 tsp saffron powder
1/2–1 tbsp ground cardamom
1/2 tsp freshly grated nutmeg
1 tsp rose water
oil, for deep-frying

Preparation time: approx. 20 minutes
(excluding standing time)
763 cal/3202 kJ

■ How to do it:

Mix both the flours with the yeast, the yoghurt and approximately 9 fl oz–18 fl oz (250–500 ml) water and stir into a rough dough. Allow to stand for 2 hours. While waiting heat up 18 fl oz (500 ml) water with the sugar until it turns to a thick syrup, stirring occasionally. Stir in the saffron, cardamom, nutmeg and the rose water. Heat up the oil in a deep fryer. Add the dough to an icing bag and squirt rings into the oil. Cook until the dough becomes crispy and brown, take out of the oil and dry on a kitchen towel. Coat the deep-fried rings in the syrup and serve on a plate.

Rice flour

Rice is the main source of nutrition in Indian cooking and comes in many forms. Flour in particular is made out of cheaper rice sorts. It is a coarse flour with a mild aroma. It can be purchased ready made, but many women in India grind it themselves to have it fresh.

1 Cook the water and sugar together into a thick syrup.

2 Stir in the spices and the rose water.

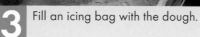

3 Fill an icing bag with the dough.

4 Coat the deep-fried rings in the syrup.

INDEX OF RECIPES